*'A most remarkable old lady'*

# MOTHER FOR PEACE: Lucy Behenna

LUCY BEHENNA was a most remarkable old lady. She lived in a retirement home in Sussex, was a member of the Society of Friends, had no money beyond her state pension and must have been well over 80 when she died a few years ago.

She taught me a lesson or two about getting things done. Four years before she died she had two bright ideas. One was to start something called Mothers for Peace and the other was to raise enough money, and it would cost several thousand pounds, to pay for the fares for some Russian mothers to visit the United States and for some American mothers to visit the USSR.

She put the idea to me and, at my patronising best, I told her that the ideas were great but that she would have to leave them to someone else to carry through. After all on a pension in a retirement home how can you, Lucy, expect to be able to manage? She sensibly ignored my ridiculous advice and got on with the job with quiet determination. Mothers for Peace still exists and that bridge building exchange visit did take place but it took Lucy many letters and much effort.

—Bruce Kent in the *Catholic Herald*
8 January, 1988

*Photo: D. Andrews*

*'A most remarkable old lady'*

# MOTHER FOR PEACE:
# Lucy Behenna

by
Sheila Ward

Published for
MOTHERS FOR PEACE
by
QUAKER HOME SERVICE
and QUAKER PEACE & SERVICE

First published July 1989
by Quaker Home Service
and Quaker Peace & Service
Friends House, Euston Road, London NW1 2BJ


ISBN 0 85245 219 5

Printed in Great Britain in Palatino 10/12
by Headley Brothers Ltd, Invicta Press
Ashford, Kent and London

# Contents

Foreword x
Introduction 1
1 Childhood 3
2 Early teaching days 7
3 Encounter with poverty 12
4 War years 20
5 Dorothy 23
6 Post-war years 28
7 Peace women 33
8 Retirement 47
9 Exchange visits with the Soviet Union 55
10 Ifield 59
11 A new initiative: Mothers for Peace 64
12 The first stages 71
13 Selection of mothers 76
14 Mothers in the Soviet Union, 1981 79
15 Mothers in the USA 84
16 Return visit 89
17 Tears and rainbows 96
18 Coping with old age 104
19 Visits to the USSR, 1984 109
20 Visit to the USA, 1984 118
21 Peace garden 129
References 140
Further reading 141

# Acknowledgements

I am very grateful to Mothers for Peace for entrusting me with the writing of this book. It has been a most enriching experience.

There is little recorded about Lucy on any official files. Almost all her letters and diaries were destroyed at the time of her death because there were no relatives and it was not thought at the time that they would be of interest. Inevitably many of her contemporaries are no longer living and Lucy herself was someone who lived very much in the present and rarely talked about the past. So in writing this account of Lucy's life I am sadly aware that much of her experience will remain for ever hidden. However, I am most grateful to the many friends who have told me of their memories of Lucy and have remembered things which she told them about herself. I should like to thank Marion Mansergh, Pat Dale and Grace Crookall-Greening for their help and encouragement.

I should also like to thank Mary Addey, Muriel Ardley, Cathy Ashton, Charles and Margaret Ashwell, Richenda Barbour, Sylvia Bond, Eileen Brock, Joan Castwood, Len and Isobel Clarke, Marjorie Coles, Sybil Cookson, Margaret Cooper, John Cox, Margaret Curwen, Joan Darnton, Alun Davies, Sylvia Dingwall, Miss K. Dowdell, Roy Farrant, David Firth, Maude and Norah Gibbins, Veida Greer, Elma Harland, Ronald Harris, Denis Hayes, Alan and Caroline Herring, Margaret Hutchinson, Bruce Kent, Maria Khristoforovna, Margaret Kohler, Dairo Lean Smith, Margaret MacColl, Ross Maddocks, Ruth Martin, Kathleen Matthews, Henry Mettleman, Elsie Mitchell, Marina Moskvina, Dick Nettleton, Jim Norman, Rose Paton, Else Pickvance, Sherry Phillips, Sheila Ragg, Duncan Rees, Ted Rogers, A. D. Rowland, Connie Seifert, Irene Stevens, Reg Tait, Marjorie Thorpe, Grahame Todd, Jan Toms, Linda Townsend, Alison Tyas, Isobel Weedon, Steve Whitehead and Sue Wolf. I am most grateful for the help given by librarians at Friends House Library and at Grange House, Neasden, and to the British-Soviet Friendship Society.

My grateful thanks also to my husband, Alec and my daughter Jennifer for all their help and encouragement. Warmest thanks too to Elizabeth Cave for her sympathetic checking and editing.

In the latter part of the book I have quoted extensively from Mothers for Peace accounts of visits to the USSR and the USA as well as visits from overseas mothers to Britain. Much of this writing was anonymous and I should like to thank those concerned.

# Foreword

Mothers for Peace is glad to be part of this joint publication with QHS and QPS of the life story of Lucy Behenna. We are grateful to mother for peace Sheila Ward for researching and writing it and welcome it as a loving tribute to a life in the service of peace and as part of our continuing work. The foundations Lucy and Marion Mansergh laid have proved firm ground on which to build our still growing organization. The inspired simplicity of their original idea remains our focus.

As this biography is published Mothers for Peace looks to the 1990s, finding in the changing international political climate that the work of trust building is ever more important.

We now have a UK mailing list of almost four hundred and international contacts in twenty-six countries. Growth in numbers has required the organization of a committee and officers but we continue to work in non-hierarchical ways, reaching agreement by consensus, listening to each other.

The visits we arrange to this country now often include an opportunity for round-table discussion with the whole group. We find this valuable and rewarding and are glad that some invitations we receive now have this dual format.

It is a joy to us that our way of working and our aims are respected and acknowledged by official organizations in East Europe, and that in the USA the women who responded to the first visit and those involved since continue to work with us for peace and international understanding.

The building of trust and confidence on this individual basis may be slow and the results hard to quantify but it is our experience and belief that each visit, each delegation, each report read, each talk given makes a ripple and the ripples spread—world peace *will* come.

If you would like more information about Mothers for Peace, please write to:
Beryl Milner, National Co-ordinator, 70 Station Road, Burley-in-Wharfedale, Ilkley, West Yorkshire LS29 7NG.

# *Introduction*

Various factors attracted me to find out more about Lucy Behenna.

Over the past few years I have become very interested in the potential of women for healing both broken bodies and a broken world. This century women have a far longer life expectation than ever before and after child-bearing and family-raising is over, they may have twenty or thirty years more productive life ahead of them. By the time they are fifty they have an accumulated life experience which can be of real value to the society in which they live. This wisdom has always been there, but women have not lived so long in previous centuries and this is the first time in the history of the world that substantial numbers of older women have had the education, confidence and opportunity to reappraise their experience in terms of their own reality rather than having a male theoretical interpretation thrust upon them. Increasingly, women are exploring the meaning of life by comparing their own experience with that of other women, very often using a book—and especially a biography—as a starting point. I hope this account of the life of Lucy Behenna may also serve as such a catalyst. Personally I have learnt much from Lucy during my year's research and from encountering directly or indirectly many of those associated with her who have themselves lived extremely interesting and valuable lives.

Lucy seems to me to illustrate many factors which need further exploration. She produced her most creative work when well into her eighties. Having worked for peace most of her life by protest and by urging the government to act, she realized late in life that peace will come through the actions of ordinary people like ourselves and acted on this with far-reaching results.

Although she never married or had children of her own, she was open to the kind of relationship which can produce creativity in other spheres and she observed in her own life as a teacher the enormous power of maternal love.

Many biographies are written about women who had adventurous lives packed with incident. Lucy's own sister Dorothy had a far more eventful life than she did. Yet the interesting thing about Lucy is the way that she was able to transform incidents of everyday life into moments of inspiration. This culminated in her founding, with Marion Mansergh, Mothers for Peace.

Her significance lies in the fact that she did not merely preach an idea, but she actively involved herself in enabling others to carry out the project and proved the wisdom of her conviction to the extent that the project then began to grow from its own impetus. Her organization is founded on belief in the power of love and the ability of women to cooperate for peace. She acted on her idea with indomitable courage and perseverance.

So what lay behind this diminutive woman who inspired so much affection, belief and action in her cause?

# 1
# *Childhood*

At the end of the last century our planet had been fully explored and world wide communication was becoming a possibility. The Victorian father still ruled supreme in England. Yet the first glimmerings of something new in the history of the world were beginning to appear. The Education Act of 1870 gave all children, for the first time, the opportunity to read and write. In 1880 free school education was available and in 1891 it was made compulsory. The first generation of mostly literate women appeared, whose daughters and granddaughters would first of all learn to see the world through men's eyes and then would start to articulate their own perceptions and feelings. A minority of women had already been able to develop intellectually and apply their minds to the world situation. In 1872 an American woman, Julia Ward Howe, who had been converted to pacifism by the horrors of the Franco-Prussian War, which had caused mass starvation in Paris, went to Europe to try and organize an international women's peace congress. She failed to do so because at that time many women thought it was not their business to interfere. However this first known international women's peace initiative held in it the seeds of growth in the following century.

It was into this world of new beginnings that Lucy was born.

Behenna is a Cornish name but both Lucy's parents were born in London in the year 1873. Her mother, Lucy Heather Leslie Bailey, was a seamstress who probably specialized in embroidered lingerie. There were several dressmaking agencies in North London at this time and the girls worked from 8.30 am to 8 pm for three or four shillings a week. Often the work could be brought home and was paid for on a piece-work basis. A friend of Lucy's described her mother as 'a saint (although she would never have thought of herself in this way)'. She was barely five foot high but very strong.

Richard John Behenna was a strict and upright man. Both he and his wife were Anglicans and 'really good not just to their friends, but also to their relatives'. Richard was a gas governor maker journeyman (a qualified artisan) at a time when London was lit by gas lamps, each with a governor controlling the flow of gas to the burner. A testimonial to his efficiency and helpfulness still exists in the shape of two china figurines presented to him by the Doulton factory when he came to their rescue with repairs. One of these represents a lavender maid and one a midinette (a Parisian shop-girl) and they became part of the Behenna household.

The young couple were living in lodgings with Mrs Bishop at 11 Milton Road (now rebuilt as Milton Grove), South Hornsey, when on February 29th, 1896 Lucy was born. She was named after her mother and her aunt Clara. Life was probably hard for the Behennas at this time and it is likely that Lucy suffered from rickets. As a result of this her small stature was accentuated by having bow legs and in later years her legs were crippling and painful.

Three years later in August 1899 another baby daughter was born at the same address. Dorothy had a deformity of the neck which pulled her head over to one side. Throughout her school days this was never corrected and led to her becoming spoiled by the family. Lucy was very defensive on behalf of her sister and would say 'Oh let me do it', rushing to help Dorothy at her slightest need.

Their mother often used to call Lucy 'Mally' and described her as a 'fly by night'. Her school friends called her a 'spitfire', with long black hair to her waist and bandy legs. Although she was small she was strong and courageous and on one occasion, when a schoolboy taunted her about the height of her mother, he found himself on the ground being punched by a furious Lucy. A school master, putting his head round the door to see what was going on, was too astonished to give Lucy more than a mild reprimand.

Lucy's junior school had a strong Anglican tradition. 'Everyone is your sister and brother,' she was taught. There was a home for unmarried mothers next door to the school and she was taught that these were 'naughty people' who had gone astray, but they were still her sisters. Before long there was a knock at the front door of this house and the warden opened it to find Lucy on the doorstep. 'I've come to see my sisters,' she announced. 'But who are your sisters? What's your name?' the woman demanded angrily. 'I'm Lucy Behenna and they are all my sisters,' replied Lucy sweetly, holding out a box of chocolates. 'I've brought them some chocolates.' 'What nonsense!' the woman snapped. 'Where do you come from?' Lucy explained that she went to the school next door and that she had been told that these girls were her sisters. She proffered the box of chocolates again. Understanding dawned and the woman took the chocolates telling Lucy not to come and bother them any more. She must have told the school about this because Lucy was scolded for her behaviour. 'I puzzled about it for ages afterwards,' Lucy recalled. 'I couldn't understand.'

When she was fourteen Lucy won a scholarship to Maida Vale High School. She was an excellent pupil although never very good at French. Her main interest was in geography and the Head realized that here was a pupil with potential and helped her with extra tuition so that she was able to go to a teacher training college.

John Behenna was very ambitious for both his daughters. Apart from her school work, Lucy also took an interest in public affairs, but her father was very angry on one occasion when she stayed out late to attend a public meeting in London.

# 2
# *Early Teaching Days*

While Lucy was doing her teacher training the First World War broke out. In later years Lucy told several people that she had a fiancé who was killed during the war, but unfortunately we know nothing about him. She often spoke of the many women of her generation who had been denied motherhood by the killing of an enormous number of men during this time. Apart from her own personal loss, Lucy must have been appalled at the human wastage and the realization which came to all in Britain at that time, that war was not the romantic glory of a Rupert Brooke poem but the horror of death in the muddy trenches of Ypres and other European battlefields. We know too that the events taking place in the Soviet Union during these years made a great impact on her thinking.

Lucy gained her Board of Education Certificate in 1917. During the next nine years she lived at home and taught geography in London schools. One of these schools was Nicholas Gibson School in The Highway, East London, and another was Senior Street School in North Paddington.

Senior Street School had been built in 1915 on demolished housing land. It was an excellent building, serving an area of extreme deprivation and presented a sharp contrast to the conditions under which most of the children lived. The streets surrounding the school were described by a contemporary writer as 'among the most degraded in London'. Middle class families had moved out of the area when Paddington station was built and their large old houses were inhabited by the working classes who had been evicted by the station builders. Several families usually lived in one house. The work of the school was as much social as educational.

During the 1920s a scheme started for the exchange of teachers within the British Empire. Lucy applied for an exchange with an Australian teacher. She was doubtful whether her experience would be sufficient to qualify her but she persevered and in August 1926 set sail for the other side of the world.

Lucy was very keen to teach aboriginal children and it was arranged that she should go to a small school in the outback north of Sydney. She recounted later how she arrived in Sydney without knowing anyone and then was sent off by herself to find her way to the school. This took several days and she was eventually rescued by a sheep farmer who brought her to her new home. Up to the end of her life she had a watercolour painting on her wall of Govett's Leap, Black Heath, and it seems likely that this is where she taught. The school and the room in which she taught were on stilts and she was very aware of the danger from poisonous snakes, relating how one day she summoned a man to come and kill a large snake under the house only to discover that it was not poisonous after all. While there, she was taught to ride by a local sheep farmer. On one occasion the horse threw her. Lucy thought she had broken her arm, but her teacher was only concerned that his wife should not discover what he had been doing and was not in the least bothered about Lucy's injury. She was evidently well liked by the children and told how on one occasion, when she had decided to give them a longer lunch break than usual, one of the older children came to warn her that a train had just gone by giving three blasts on its whistle. This signal meant that the school inspector was on board, and enabled them to rush back into the classroom before he arrived.

After she left this school Lucy spent a short time teaching in Sydney and then set off for home through Canada. Here she stayed with friends before travelling back across the

Atlantic. In the 1920s it was no mean feat to have travelled round the world like this, especially for a young and comparatively penniless schoolteacher.

It was soon after she returned from Canada that she went with some friends on holiday to a coastal resort in Belgium. Here she met a French priest from the Papal Nunciature in Brussels. He was a highly educated man from a wealthy French family and he must have found Lucy a stimulating companion after her experience in other parts of the world. Likewise she responded to someone with a less parochial outlook than the family and friends to whom she had returned in London. It was clearly a creative relationship which in other circumstances could have developed into something more. As it was, when Lucy returned to London he would come over and take her out to dinner in expensive hotels. Lucy recalled many years later that this was the opportunity she had had to become a mother. Although he was not prepared to leave the priesthood and get married he desperately wanted a child and asked Lucy if she would be the mother—but on his terms. This she was not prepared to do. Perhaps too an essential part of the man she loved was his celibate vocation, which she may have recognized engendered a spiritual rather than a physical creativity.

In 1925 the Behenna family had moved into a house in Kensal Green at 88 Kempe Road. It seems to have been a very happy home full of visiting friends and relations who all called Lucy's mother 'Mum' or 'Mumsy' and were rather in awe of her father. 'Mumsy' used to enjoy going window-shopping with some of their friends. This was an occupation which Lucy and Dorothy spurned.

Lucy had her tonsils out at home in about 1929. A friend recalls visiting her to find a room full of people, with such a strong smell of anaesthetic that someone fainted and had to be revived by pricking with a hat-pin. The owner of the hat-pin bewailed that her hat was coming off, Lucy was crying to her mother that she didn't want to die yet, everyone was fussing over her and in the commotion someone remembered to comfort the dog.

When Dorothy started her nursing training she at last had an operation to straighten her neck and this must have greatly increased her confidence. She first of all trained as a V.A.D. Dorothy was also running a Christian youth club near Marble Arch where Lucy would go along to help. It was here that the sisters often encountered girls from broken homes and would bring them back to the Behenna household where they would be semi-adopted and come to regard this house as their new home. One of the protégées said that Dorothy, whom they called 'Gardy', was like a father to her, while Lucy was like a mother.

Towards the end of the 1920s Dorothy was training as a nurse at the Royal Free Hospital. It has been suggested that she fell in love with a doctor who was going out to the China Mission. Whether or not this is so, it was at this time that she encountered members of the Society of Friends and introduced Lucy. Lucy had been confirmed an Anglican when at Maida Vale High School, but both sisters were very impressed by the Quaker teaching and by their Quaker friends. They became members of Hampstead Meeting in March 1929.

After finishing her training as a nurse Dorothy trained as a midwife at Brighton and followed this with further training as a health visitor because she was interested in the social work side of health care. For a while she took a cottage near Godalming and worked at High Barn near Hascombe. Health visiting was a new job which made the other nurses feel their professional status might be challenged and working on her own was not easy.

Both sisters have been described as 'loners', but Dorothy seems to have had many more personal friends than Lucy.

So many people have said, 'Actually I was a friend of Dorothy's, but of course I knew Lucy'. Some have tried to describe the effect that Lucy had on them in terms of Lucy's goodness, dedication and honesty, which many found disquieting and which made it difficult to relate to her, although all appreciated her sense of humour and caring nature.

By 1930 the family were reasonably well off and could afford some help in the house. Mrs Behenna consulted her next door neighbours, the Elliotts, who recommended a cleaner whom they had for one day a week. Thereafter for many years this woman walked up from North Kensington one day a week to work from 9 am to 12 noon, being paid tenpence and later a shilling an hour. Sometimes in the school holidays she would bring her daughter Irene with her. Irene recalls how Lucy would talk and laugh with her in the middle downstairs room which had bookcases, a very high-seated leather settee and brown lino, chairs and rugs. As a child she noticed the likeness between Lucy and her mother: both with long hair and a bun at the back, pear-shaped faces and rosy cheeks. She was allowed to borrow books, provided they were kept clean, and was given geographical magazines. At 11 am the dining-room table was laid with a white damask table cloth and lunch, usually bread, cheese and tea were served. One day Mrs Behenna brought large tomatoes from the shops. Irene had never seen tomatoes before and had no idea how to tackle them. Lucy gave a demonstration: 'Eat it like an apple,' she said, 'Dip it in the salt at the side of your plate like this.' When Irene brought a yo-yo one day Lucy practised until she had mastered it and then bought one for herself.

During this period Lucy's father developed Parkinson's Disease and on New Year's Day 1933 he died. Perhaps John Behenna was too austere to have had a very close relationship with his daughters, but Lucy had a great respect for him. She was then thirty-six. Mrs Behenna kept the house on in Kempe Road as a home for her two daughters.

# 3
# *Encounter With Poverty*

Since 1926 some members of the Society of Friends had been active in working for conciliation in the industrial crisis in the South Wales coal fields. During the early 1930s Lucy joined a group of these Quakers to live for a short period in a very deprived mining village.

The aim was to live with local people as members of the community and bring help and religious teaching to those with whom they lived. The conditions were very tough and one of the worst aspects was the dirt and stench. Some Friends who had come from middle-class households found this very hard to take and at first put it down to ignorance and the kind of mental attitude which went with lack of education. 'Perhaps these people did not realize that they smelled.' But as time went on the hard facts of the situation sunk in. When there was no money to buy soap and washing powder, cleanliness was a major problem. On a cold winter's morning when it was necessary to go out and break the ice, bring in water, light a fire and heat it before having a wash, it was all too easy to think, 'Well, I'll maybe give it a miss this morning and no-one will notice'. And the helpers found themselves falling into this trap too, until after a while to their horror they realized that they too were smelling like the others. This experience made a great impact on Lucy. She said later, 'I started to realize that actually the conditions were creating the visual appearance. Grubby-looking clothes, all those things were not a mental attitude at all. They weren't to do with lack of education so much as lack of facilities. It was really a hard lesson to learn and quite an enlightening thing. The amazing realization crept round everybody and some of these people who had been talking about the smells and the dirt just gradually stopped talking about it because they realized that it was happening to them too. The realization came that poverty is something economic and practical. If you haven't got the money you can't purchase the goods. You can't purchase those things you need to entertain the mind either. Just being able to get fish and chips every day and wood for the fire does not mean you're living . . . you need a cultural background as well'.

Lucy had encountered poverty in London but this depth of deprivation was a new experience for her. At the same time she was tremendously impressed by the cooperation, resilience and cheerfulness of the people and the mutual support within the community. This was probably a major contributory factor which led to her later becoming a Communist.

The other factor was undoubtedly the events which were taking place in the Soviet Union. Reports of the revolution reached the English public together with the exciting new ideas of Marx, Engels and Lenin. It seemed to Lucy that despite the bloodshed of the revolution a new society of social justice was being forged, in which the terrible poverty she had experienced would be wiped out and with men and women working together throughout the world a new possibility of peace would emerge. To someone who felt so passionately about peace and social justice these new ideas must have seemed relevant and full of hope. In 1938 she visited Moscow for the first time.

Back in London her work was increasingly among the poor and unemployed. It seems likely that she was influenced directly or indirectly by three remarkable women who had also been working in such areas for many years: Mary Hughes, Sylvia Pankhurst and Christine Greenfield.

Mary Hughes was thirty-six years older than Lucy to the day. She too had her birthday on February 29th. Mary was born into a wealthier family than Lucy's: her father was a county court judge and author of *Tom Brown's Schooldays* but he was a caring man and did much to alleviate the conditions of the less well-off. He was a leader of the Christian Socialist movement and played a part in setting up cooperatives. After working as housekeeper for her uncle and learning something of the oppression and misery of 'the Poor House' and the Cottage Hospitals, Mary inherited enough money to be independent when he died in 1891. Her father died the following year. She then went to live with her sister in Stepney where her brother-in-law was a curate. She immediately plunged into the life there, seeing worse poverty than anything she had yet encountered. She became a member of the Board of Guardians for Stepney and worked among the homeless, the sick, the children and the unemployed. Gradually she came to realize that in order to relate to these people she must live as one of them and not return to the comfort of the vicarage each evening. In 1912 this instinct was reinforced by the tragic drowning of her brother-in-law and sister in the *Titanic*. Mary was now homeless herself and lived for a while with two sisters in a small room at the top of a building.

Mary was disgusted with the attitude of the churches in the First World War. She came in contact with several Quakers who worked with her in Stepney and she herself became a member of the Society of Friends in 1918. By now she was living in a small council flat with a notice on the door saying, 'Walk in and if no one's in, make yourself a cup of tea'. She was not naive and had a sharp eye for con-men but on the whole she believed that 'people are wonderful if you treat them as wonderful'. Mary lived very simply as a vegetarian, and her distinctive feature was the long red cloak she wore. She was dismayed at the terrible unemployment and ensuing misery which followed the war. She became a Labour councillor in Stepney and a magistrate so that she could speak for her neighbours more effectively. She never needed to go round canvassing. She was known and trusted and always topped the poll. Most of her time was spent with those who had no votes. As a magistrate she would sometimes pay the fines herself because she sympathized with the accused. In the General Strike of 1926 when the government defeated the trade unions, Mary's faith in the Labour Party was shaken and she eventually became a Communist though always prophesying disaster for communism unless it learnt to embrace Christianity. She was henceforth nicknamed 'Comrade' and moved to a rather disreputable public house in Vallance Road, Whitechapel, which she turned into a centre for local people to come and meet and work out their problems. She called it 'The Dewdrop Inn—for Education and Joy'. A terrible pun, but she referred to it as 'a potting shed where people could come and move on feeling stronger and more able to cope with life'.

Many people were attracted to come and help her and she let out the top floor to sociology students. The building became a centre for classes, clubs and an advice bureau. Mary herself slept in a tiny room near the door on a padded bench, but she would often give this to some homeless woman and sleep on the floor. She could not abide people fussing over her health and would say, 'So many young people are tired when they are 17. I see no reason to be tired when I am 70'. She would never allow any heating in her room and seemed oblivious to vermin. She would lead a tiny neighbourhood worship service in the basement on Sundays, attend Quaker Meeting and then lead her own unique service there in the evening bullying her friends into giving a sermon while she accompanied the singing on the harmonium. Her advice was always 'Launch out!', in other words 'Take a risk and do it now!' Mary's life and work were the same thing. What she left behind was not an organization or a system but a warm memory of caring and concern in the lives of the thousands she had helped. Mary died in 1941.

We do not know that Lucy ever met Mary Hughes but they shared a similarity of outlook and single-minded dedication to what they believed. In the Quaker/Communist milieu of the East End Lucy must surely have known of Mary and found reinforcement for her own aims and convictions.

Another woman active in the East End of London at this time was Sylvia Pankhurst. She was fourteen years older than Lucy. Unlike her mother Emmeline and her sister Christabel, Sylvia was a pacifist. She believed in working for women's suffrage by nonviolent means. She ran her own independent suffrage organization, The East London Federation of Suffragettes. She has been described as 'a melodramatic maverick, gutsy, well loved and dedicated to fighting poverty and deprivation'. Much of her energy was absorbed in running subsidized canteens, a children's nursery and a toy factory. Sylvia was also active in the campaign for equal pay for women, protesting against conscription, supporting conscientious objectors and working for peace through the Women's International League for Peace and Freedom (about which more later).

While teaching in Bethnal Green, Lucy was still living at home and in her spare time helped with a club for young unemployed people in Willesden.

The depression of the late 1920s and 1930s had brought unemployment to that part of London too. Concern was expressed at the misery of men hanging around the labour exchange in St Mary's Road in the bitter cold. A Presbyterian minister, Bill Hinsley, had taken the initiative to open his church hall across the road to provide tea and a warm place to sit for those who were waiting. From this grew the Willesden Unemployed and Social Welfare Committee who appointed as their voluntary secretary a young girl straight from college, Christine Greenfield. Christine's father was, amongst other things, the conductor of the Willesden Philharmonic Orchestra and she herself had a life-long interest in ballet. She was also a lively writer and a talented amateur painter and had just taken her BA at Kings College before volunteering for the post with the Unemployment Committee. The Committee was soon operating from two centres, raising money and able to help in cases of distress as well as giving advice and assistance. Much help was given by local organizations but its inception was opposed by the local Communist Party who did their utmost to hinder its work. The Committee protested that they were not political, only humanitarian. There was no question of charity. They aimed only to 'bring a little brightness and comfort into the lives of thousands of men who were unfortunately unemployed'. Soon after Christine took up her post as secretary, the emphasis became more on the women and children who, she realized, were suffering even more than the men. Her reaction was to appeal for a country house where mothers could go and take a rest. Before long one was offered in Hertfordshire and then another in Surrey. Christine would organize the bedding, catering and care of the children so that the mothers could have a complete rest in the country.

When she died in 1962, Christine Greenfield was described in these words: 'She was gentle, she was kind, she was patient and above all well-informed and the information and knowledge she had acquired was available to all.' Her office was described as:

> a place for healing, a place sometimes of rough justice, but however rough, justice it certainly was. It was a place of standards where standards were falling, a place of light when darkness was gathering, a place of life when death was abounding. Christine Greenfield was a paci-

> fist during the war but saw pacifism as a contribution to social revolution . . . a revolution which was to grow out of tolerance because she accepted everyone on the basis of need. She was not religious in the accepted meaning of the word, but she was profoundly spiritual and she found God in men, women and children. She was a seeker and the object of her search was beauty. She tried to discover beauty in people and when the rest of the world saw nothing beautiful in them, she did. She never married, yet children were always her passion and the love she could not give to children of her own she gave to the children of friends. Her personal troubles and triumphs were not communicated even to her friends. They were things she dealt with alone. Her life was solitary as the life of every really great person was always solitary.[1]

It seems probable that Lucy knew Christine Greenfield personally, but certainly she must have known of her work with the unemployed youth of Willesden. The minutes of Hampstead Meeting of December 1935 record that Lucy Behenna told of her work with a fellowship club for the youth of this area and asked for help from Friends. She was given their support.

The Communists were active in North London at this time. On one occasion in February 1932 they raided the vestry hall where the Public Assistance Committee was handling applications for relief and demanded relief without a means test. Communist ideas were very much in evidence and not always greeted with hostility. In October 1932 the Scottish hunger marches attracted huge crowds. Support in the Willesden area was provided by Bill Hinsley and other clergy. The hunger marchers carried red banners calling on the proletariat to join the march. The *Willesden Chronicle* began a series on 'Russia Today'. In 1934 four hundred hunger marchers from Yorkshire arrived in

Willesden on their way to the Congress of Action on February 26th. Both the Communists and the ILP regarded this Congress as the 'starting point of the mightiest mobilization of workers for action yet seen in this country'. A contingent of fifty women left Derby and South Wales and another group started from Bath. The women wore red berets and red kerchiefs and the men carried an assortment of banners and slogans. Yet on the whole it was a good humoured event. The Willesden clergy had been challenged to do as Christ would have done and they responded as in 1932 by providing accommodation. The Cooperative Women's Guild defied official Labour Party policy and came out on the side of the marchers, doing the catering and helping in other ways. The procession was led by a pipe band and escorted by mounted police and many more officers on foot. It was remarked that they were on the friendliest possible terms with the police. On their return the marchers were given a farewell concert and social in a Kensal Rise church hall where again it was emphasized that the motives of those taking part were humanitarian and not political.

# 4
# *War Years*

Until the 1930s it was still possible to hope that the 1914–18 war had been the war to end all wars, but as the decade continued the prospect of war once more loomed ahead and the Quaker Meeting to which Lucy belonged began to prepare itself for the possibility of conscription.

Lucy was passionately opposed to conscription. Through her work with the Willesden unemployed she had come to know Joseph Fleming who shared her convictions.

Joseph Fleming was a Quaker and an inspiration to all who came in contact with him. He lived with his wife in Welwyn Garden City, where he had access to land which he used for children's camps and later for agricultural work with conscientious objectors. In 1939 he was supervisor of Fellowship House, from which the Willesden Unemployed and Social Welfare Committee was run. By the time war broke out, he was in charge of the Citizens' Advice Bureau there. Although he was a pacifist, he was a strong defender of service-men's wives, campaigning against their exploitation by landlords and demanding better benefits for them and their families. For those who could not come for advice during working hours he had an evening session on Tuesdays which he held at the Behenna home in Kempe Road. During the early part of the war he wrote to the papers and spoke whenever possible on issues of social justice and especially peace. In one of his articles outlining a world federation he wrote: 'War is the most signal instance of arrested human, cultural and intellectual development.'[2]

He and Lucy together ran an advisory service for conscientious objectors from Lucy's home on Thursday evenings. Lucy put advertisements in the *Willesden Chronicle* and other local papers inviting 'men between 20 and 21 likely to be called up for military service and who object to war and military training to call any evening at 88 Kempe Road, Kensal Rise, Thursday 8pm–10pm to receive instructions how *not* to join up'.

This advisory service was in fact performing a complex task. There were three categories of non-combatant, depending on the grounds of conscience behind a man's decision to apply for exemption from military service. Many who were turned down by the tribunal decided to persevere and appeal against the decision at an Appellate Tribunal. A refusal to abide by the decision of the court resulted in imprisonment. Joseph and Lucy did more than just give advice: agricultural work-parties were arranged for conscientious objectors, moral support given to those in prison and practical support to their relatives.

Among those who attended this centre was Hugh Brock. At the beginning of the war Hugh, with his brother Ashley, printed 'seditious' leaflets which were addressed to many people, including MPs. Lucy used to take a bundle of them in her gas-mask case and post them well away from the printing works.

Most children had been evacuated from London at this time and indeed Lucy and her mother were evacuated at one point (perhaps with Lucy's school) to a place in Wales, but they soon returned. Even those who longed to have children must have hesitated to bring them into such a war-stricken world. However there were those who had hope for the future. In October 1941 the wife of one of the imprisoned conscientious objectors gave birth to a son. Joseph Fleming wrote to her: 'I know that this is the greatest event in your life shared by your charming man. You are right. You have handed on to posterity a link in the chain the distant end of which will see a wiser, happier world.'

Lucy was then forty-five. It was too late to have any children of her own.

Lucy continued her teaching during the war but it was not easy. One of the girls, finding out that Lucy was a pacifist, said that she would not be taught by her. Lucy said that she would not wish to compel her, nor would she want her examination preparation to suffer, so she would set work for her to do and hand in to save the girl from feeling the humiliation of being taught by a pacifist in wartime.

The street shelters were just outside the Behenna home in Kempe Road, but apparently they were not used much by Lucy and her mother.

Later in the war she found a number of children who had drifted back from evacuation and others who had been left behind and had no provision for schooling. She set up an informal school for them herself. She was in the East End during the worst part of the V1 and V2 bombing at the end of the war. It was at that time, when she was down in a shelter with the children, that she made the resolution which was to focus the rest of her life. She described it later: 'It was in 1945 during an air-raid. I was sitting in one of those shelters with a group of children and a buzz bomb came over—and those agonizing minutes when we waited to see if we were all going to be blown to bits or not. It came near enough to shake us but it did not harm us. I vowed then that if I came through I would work even harder for peace to see that it never happened again.'

Apart from the hazards of war-time London, Lucy and her mother had the personal anguish of not knowing what had become of Dorothy, who had been taken prisoner of war by the Japanese in 1940. Yet when the war ended and it was discovered that Dorothy was still alive and returning to England perhaps the most traumatic experience of Lucy's life was still to come, when Dorothy came home.

# 5
# *Dorothy*

Dorothy had heard something of Quaker missionary work in China while she was at the Royal Free Hospital. In 1934, Dr Lucy Harris returned from China on furlough and toured many Friends Meetings around the country vividly describing Friends' medical work in China and particularly emphasizing the need for an English nurse. Dorothy, now a trained nurse, midwife and health visitor, responded to this appeal and that autumn went to Kingsmead College at Selly Oak to train as a missionary. She completed her training at Woodbrooke, the Quaker college, and set sail for China with Lucy Harris in September 1935. She planned to spend the first year in language study and then hoped to assist with the training of nurses and become involved with village health work.

At this time China and Japan were already at war. The missionaries with whom Dorothy was to work tried to bring reconciliation, but without success. Harry Silcock had been out in China from 1907 to 1920 and had married a fellow missionary in Chengdu. He was in London from 1920 to 1938, still involved with Chinese concerns, but went out east again in 1938, going first to Japan with hopes of finding ways towards peace. Missionaries going out on a boat in 1938 had a chance meeting with Japanese fellow passengers and their conversation revealed how much these Japanese also regretted the war, feeling that it was demoralizing the Japanese people as well as destroying China. In the University of Chengdu the Friends had close contact with many Buddhists, some of whom would join them for meetings for worship. In particular there was an old teacher, Chen, a tall man with a long flowing beard, who was 'a splendid influence on the other students' and a regular attender. The missionaries were impressed by the non-military attitudes of the Chinese with whom they worked and by their reactions to the Japanese invasion on a human level. In 1939 Harry Silcock was transferred from Chengdu to Shanghai where he set up the Shanghai Centre.

Our society tends to ignore or deride the element of emotional involvement in relationships outside narrow conventional limits. It fails to affirm the diversity and depth of working relationships with their potential to inspire and energize as well as to be supportive. Harry Silcock was a charismatic man who evoked a personal response from his colleagues and Dorothy evidently appreciated the opportunity to work with him.

Dorothy began her work in Chengdu. In June that year there was a serious air-raid. The university buildings were badly damaged and a bomb dropped near a Friends' residence. Some of the university staff were killed, but the mission was safe. In November Dorothy left Chengdu, where she had been running a children's clinic, to go to help Dr Lucy Harris at the hospital in Tungchwan. She then returned to look after the Silcocks' daughter and nurse her through a difficult illness.

Evidently these years in Chengdu and Tungchwan were not easy. Dorothy found the language difficult. Besides this, she was very determined and her colleagues were equally strong-minded. A friend recalls a journey in a rickshaw when Dorothy insisted they go one way and her fellow passenger insisted that the other was the right one. Dorothy won the argument but was proved wrong. Since this was recalled nearly fifty years later it must have been quite an argument.

Just as the war in the west was beginning, Dorothy found herself in Shanghai on her way home on furlough and became involved in setting up a 'reception home' for destitute children organized by the Volunteer Service Scheme at the Shanghai Centre. As a result of the unsettled conditions in China there were large numbers of lost children. The provision of a home where they could be cared for gave an opportunity to investigate their individual needs and decide on a suitable destination or form of employment. From its inauguration Dorothy supervised this home with a Chinese member of the Central Office staff, Evelyn Mary Chan. The actual social work was done by the Shanghai Municipal Council. During this period Dorothy wrote:

> As I write the voices of our children drift in to me from their dining room for it is supper time. I do wish you could see it all. The house when we first came over was so dirty, but now, so busy have we been, that it almost sparkles with cleanliness. The kiddies do their share by keeping the room they use clean themselves—an early morning chore—and how they enjoy doing it! On Saturday they have measure pressed down, for we turn them loose to scour corners. No cleaning was done here for a good two years so we have an accumulation of various kinds. Miss Chan is responsible for the time-table both of work and study and a grand job she is making of it. The children seem to be thoroughly contented and yet full of life, and one at least is overflowing with harmless mischief.
>
> The histories of these little people are sad in the extreme, but not in every case bad. Three of them have simply got lost and cannot make contact with their parents. The business of losing one's children as one loses one's purse takes a bit of getting used to, but in Shanghai it really does happen. Had we not taken them, they must have either begged to live or remained at a police station in the foulest conditions indefinitely. To use Miss Chan's phrase: 'We shall spare the tears of the parents when they know.'

> We had the head of the Child Protection Department in for a few moments recently and she really seemed almost too overcome to be able to find words to express her appreciation of this effort. She has dreamed for a long time, I gather, of this kind of place to which she could send her children.

After this delay in Shanghai, Dorothy once more set off for home, knowing that she would need surgery while she was in England. She had only just set sail, however, when the attack on Pearl Harbour initiated a global war. The ship on which she was travelling was captured by the Japanese and she was dumped on the quay at Manila to spend the rest of the war in captivity. For a few months she remained in Manila nursing Filipino bomb victims in a temporary hospital. Each Sunday she kept her silent Meeting alone in her cubicle witnessing to her peace testimony by expressing pity for Japanese pilots burnt to death when their planes were brought down. There were Americans interned with her and she was not very popular for taking this attitude. She was allowed more freedom than most prisoners, perhaps because she was a nurse. She would never say a word against the Japanese. One elderly Japanese officer used to salute and bow to her in the street. Some of the American prisoners were medical personnel and it became apparent that the surgery which Dorothy needed could no longer be delayed. She underwent a hysterectomy in very primitive conditions. When she recovered from this she spent the rest of her captivity looking after an elderly woman missionary.

Eventually the war ended. The Americans entered Manila, releasing the prisoners. (Dorothy questioned why all their guards had to be killed.) In March 1945 Lucy and her mother received the glad news that Dorothy was safe. She was in very poor health however and weighed only six stone. Then came one of the worst moments of Lucy's life.

She and her mother had planned to go away for a holiday and they telephoned the Foreign Office to find out when Dorothy's ship was due so that they would be sure to be back in time. For some reason the ship arrived early. Instead of the wonderful homecoming which she had anticipated, Dorothy arrived to find an empty house. Lucy felt that Dorothy never forgave her for this and she seemed to spend the rest of her life trying to compensate.

Dorothy went to Woodbrooke to recuperate and underwent a mastectomy. But, as Lucy admiringly recorded later, she remained faithful in her desire to help prevent suffering. When she recovered she accepted a scholarship to train as a Child Welfare Officer and spent the following two years in London visiting homes on behalf of an adoption society.

The other immediate effect of Dorothy's homecoming for Lucy occurred because her sister believed that communism was incompatible with being a Quaker. It was in anticipation of this reaction that in April 1945 Lucy resigned from membership of the Society of Friends.

# 6
# *Post-War Years*

A friend who used to go along and help with the garden in Kempe Road after the war described the Behenna household as 'like the home of three dwarfs'. They were all very energetic, quick-moving and outspoken women with rosy cheeks. Lucy was the tallest of the three with short brown hair and often wearing brown. Their mother wore long black skirts to the ground. Dorothy was usually in navy blue, often wearing a nurse's cap. 'None of them seemed to have much interest in men,' he commented, although others have remarked on Lucy's attractiveness and her sparkle in men's company.

Lucy was fifty in 1946, nevertheless when she decided that she wanted to be able to teach science as well as geography, she set to work to get her science O-levels. Later on, when she wanted to teach needlework, she worked for a City and Guilds diploma. She then made all the covers for her furniture.

Dorothy found it difficult to settle in London. She used to attend Watling and Edgware Meeting regularly and spoke frequently. Soon she began to think of working in Surrey again and in 1953 she and her mother moved down to Godalming where they lived in a pleasant house in Tuesley Road. Dorothy planted bamboos at the bottom of the garden to remind her of China. For a while she travelled up to London every day but then found work locally at Meath House for epileptic women.

Meanwhile Lucy moved into a small second-floor flat in Ebury Street near Victoria station. It was very convenient, especially when she left Fleet Road School, Hampstead, and moved to a newly formed girls' comprehensive at Norwood. Here she taught science and biology. Her colleagues recall that she was a good teacher because she was interesting and respected, not because she was authoritarian.

During the summer holidays Lucy would accompany some of the eleven- and twelve-year-olds from Norwood on a week's visit to Colwyn Bay. They would go up by coach and stay in a hotel, visiting such places as Liverpool Cathedral, the docks and Welsh castles.

However, Lucy's vow in the air-raid shelter, that she would devote her life to working for peace, was not forgotten. Like so many others, she must have been appalled by the implications of the atomic bomb at the end of the war, by the subsequent hydrogen bomb and the ensuing nuclear tests. In 1950 the British Peace Committee claimed more than a million signatures to the Stockholm Peace Appeal. The Appeal concluded with these words:

> We demand the unconditional prohibition of the atomic weapon as a weapon of aggression and mass annihilation of people, and that strict international control for the implementation of this decision be established. We shall consider as a war criminal that government which first employs atomic weapons against any country.

Many ignored this appeal because it was backed by the Communist-led World Peace Conference. The Labour Party even added the BPC to its list of proscribed organizations. Nevertheless there were many protests about nuclear tests and a demonstration at Aldermaston where the research establishment was then being built. In October 1952 Britain tested her first atomic bomb; in November America tried a 10-megaton hydrogen bomb (equal in explosive power to 10 million tons of high explosive—far more than the total power of all explosives used by all sides in the Second World War). In August 1953 Russia tested her first H-bomb. Most traumatic of all was the US H-bomb test at Bikini Atoll in the Pacific during March 1954; a Japanese fishing boat eighty miles away was contaminated by radio-active fallout from the bomb. All the crew were sick and one died. In April 1954 a new movement was started—the Hydrogen Bomb National Campaign—and in July 1955 Bertrand Russell and Albert Einstein issued a manifesto signed by eleven internationally prominent scientists, nine of them Nobel prize winners, who described the massive genetic damage that could be caused by nuclear weapons. The manifesto concluded: 'Shall we put an end to the human race, or shall mankind renounce war?'

It is probable that Lucy attended a meeting of the Women's Cooperative Guild at Golders Green in March 1955, where the radiation risks from H-bomb tests were discussed. As a result of this meeting, Gertrude Fishwick, a retired civil servant and ex-suffragette, started and ran the Golders Green Committee for the Abolition of Nuclear Weapons Tests. Similar groups sprang up all over the country and in February 1957 a National Committee for the Abolition of Nuclear Weapons Tests (NCANWT) was formed to coordinate the efforts of more than a hundred local groups. In November 1957 J. B. Priestley wrote an article for the *New Statesman* entitled 'Britain and the Nuclear Bomb'. This drew such an enormous response that the editor, Kingsley Martin, proposed a meeting with the idea of forming a mass movement against nuclear weapons. It was decided that NCANWT should be the nucleus for this new venture and the sponsors and officers of this committee were invited to a meeting at the house of Canon John Collins of St Paul's Cathedral with about fifty others. Among those present were Bertrand Russell, Rose Macaulay, Sir Julian Huxley, Bishop Bell of Chichester, Michael Foot, Sir Richard Acland, Ritchie Calder, James Cameron, Arthur Gosse (Quaker Chairman of NCANWT), Dr Sheila Jones and Peggy Duff, who had convened the meeting. This was followed by a public meeting in Central Hall, Westminster, and the forming of a new organisation—the Campaign for Nuclear Disarmament (CND)—with aims extending beyond a ban on nuclear weapon tests. Bertrand Russell became president and Peggy Duff organizing secretary.

Hugh Brock, who had been one of the conscientious objectors with whom Lucy had worked during the war, was now editor of *Peace News*. He had organized the 1952 Aldermaston demonstration and suggested a four-day march to Aldermaston for Easter 1958. It was organized by Pat Arrowsmith. On this occasion the CND symbol was first used. This was designed by Gerald Holtom as a composite of the semaphore signal for the letters N and D. He also saw the central motif as an indication of a human being in despair—the circle represented the world, the black background, eternity. Eric Austen who made the first badge of the symbol subsequently found that the 'gesture of despair' motif has historically represented the death of man and the circle symbolized the unborn child.

The march, which began in sunshine on Good Friday morning from Trafalgar Square, continued through the cold and rain of Saturday into snow storms on Sunday (when numbers dropped to 300) to end in triumph in Aldermaston on Monday with a column of 4,000 people. The following year the direction was reversed starting from Aldermaston with 10,000 people and finishing in Trafalgar Square with about 20,000.

Meanwhile CND had set up its office near Fleet Street. Canon Collins spoke of a 'short sharp campaign' and most of those who set up CND assumed that its aims would be achieved by winning over the Labour Party and then helping it to victory. At first the campaign did indeed enjoy the support of the Labour Party, despite the fact that it was essentially a non-political movement whose sole aim was to persuade people that the atomic and similar armaments were totally wrong and should be abolished. For the first few years CND gained increasing support, but then during the 1960s numbers fell as other organizations such as the Anti-Vietnam War campaign demanded public support. Lucy worked loyally for CND throughout this period, going into the office to give what help she could and also supporting various women's peace movements.

It is relevant at this point to look back at the history of women's peace movements since the beginning of the century.

# 7
# *Peace Women*

Emmeline Pethick Lawrence, on a speaking tour of the USA early in the century, emphasized the good influence that the 'mothering instinct' would have on international politics. She wrote in *Harper's Weekly:* 'It is vital to the deepest interests of the human race that the mother-half of humanity should now be admitted into the ranks of articulate democracies of the world in order to . . . enable them to combine the more effectively in their own defence against the deadly machinery of organized destruction.' She foresaw a 'world-wide movement for constructive and creative peace such as the world has never seen'.

In the early years of this century when Lucy was still at school, the women's suffrage movement was active and growing in strength. The movement has usually been represented as a single-minded campaign for the vote as a right to which women are entitled. In fact the vote was seen as a means to bring other reforms about, not an end in itself. As the prospect of a European war drew near, the suffrage campaigners also became increasingly involved in working for peace by negotiation, although with increasing despair that nothing could be achieved without the vote.

In 1913 there had been an international conference of women's suffrage societies in Budapest largely organized by a Hungarian called Rosika Schwimmer. In Britain at the beginning of the war it was she who was a prime mover in rallying women to the cause of peace, suggesting that a personal approach be made to all the political leaders involved. This was not to be. When war broke out Rosika was increasingly under pressure as an enemy alien and left England for America.

Also in Britain at the beginning of the war was a Swiss

woman, Lucy Thoumaian, who wanted to organize a thousand women to make their way to the front to 'fling themselves between the contending armies'. 'The war was man-made, it must be woman-undone,' she told Sylvia Pankhurst.

Through the international suffrage movement links between women of many countries had been formed, and it was on this foundation that it was proposed to hold an international conference of women in 1915 in the Hague, to explore ways to end the war and find grounds on which a lasting peace could be based. Linking work for peace with the women's movement seemed clear and obvious to many women: it was all a fight against oppression. The initiative for an international congress had been taken by Dutch suffragists when they saw the plight of Belgian refugees pouring into their country. Aletta Jacobs, the leader of the Dutch delegation at the Hague Congress, said:

> We women judge war differently from men. Men consider in first place, the economic results, the cost in money, the loss or gain to national commerce and industries, the extension of power. . . . we women consider above all the damage to the race resulting from war and the grief and the pain and the misery it entails.

Here again Rosika Schwimmer played a major part. Although 180 women from Britain had intended to be present they were prevented by passport refusal and shipping blockades from getting there so that only two British women arrived. However, there were women from all the European countries and from America. There was a ban on discussing the cause of the war but they looked to the future and realized that the Women's International Congress might have a part to play in bringing the war to an end. The warring nations were too locked into conflict to be able to ask for any mediation from the neutral countries. The neutral countries were each afraid of offering mediation lest it was to their detriment and lest they might even get drawn into the war. Europe had been pulled piecemeal over the brink into war by a network of secret pacts and alliances and there was no international structure to deal with such an unprecedented situation. The women however decided that if they could send personal envoys to the leading statesmen of each warring nation and then persuade the neutral countries to organize a joint approach peace might ensue.

Not all the women were sure about this proposal and the resolution was hanging in the balance when Rosika saved the day with an impassioned speech in which she said: 'Brains they say have ruled the world until today. If brains have brought us to what we are now, I think it is time to allow our hearts to speak. When our sons are killed by millions, let us mothers only try to do good by going to kings and emperors without any other danger than refusal.' Accordingly thirteen women in two groups set off to travel Europe and interview statesmen in fourteen capitals in thirty-five separate visits. It was an astonishing project in war-torn Europe. They gave neutral governments information on what warring politicians were thinking. They were also able to convey the increasing willingness of neutral countries to play a more positive part in resolving the situation. The project finally fell through because of a lack of communication and the belief of the American women that President Wilson could be the one to mediate rather than the statesmen of the Scandinavian countries and Holland. As we now know, Wilson delayed for so long that it was too late and eventually, instead of mediating, he brought America into the war on the side of the Allies. However the women's peace initiative had paved the way for further peace progress and although they suffered hardship and indignity on their journeys they were, on the whole, treated with respect and courtesy by the leaders themselves. The Austrian foreign minister said that the women's peace proposals were the first sane words he had heard uttered in his office in the last six months. The Swedish foreign minister applauded the women for taking such an initiative and attempting to break the collective paralysis.

The Hague Peace Congress also produced a proposal for making peace based on twenty principles. This was handed to President Wilson and to other leaders and in fact it bore a remarkable resemblance to the fourteen-point plan which Wilson finally produced from the League of Nations conference at the end of the war.

Throughout the war period those who were trying to find an end to fighting were constantly being reviled as traitors and were having to promote the cause of internationalism without mentioning the word 'peace'. Britain and Russia were allies fighting Germany in the First World War as well as the second, and the October Revolution in Russia in 1917 was greeted by all internationally-minded women as a further step on the road to peace.

Although Russia was conquered by Germany, the Allies were finally victorious in November 1918. The Women's International Congress had hoped to meet at the same time and in the same place as the official peace congress. They had assumed that it would be held on neutral territory but it was not. It was held in Paris and the Germans, Hungarians and Austrians were not included. This the women could not tolerate, realizing that such behaviour would only pave the way for future war. They met in Zurich just as the terms of the official peace proposals were coming out; there were English women sitting with German women in the front row. Only two French delegates were present at the beginning of the conference and the most dramatic moment probably came on the final morning when the third French delegate appeared from a devastated region of the Ardennes. Spontaneously Lida Gustava Heymann rose from the platform and embraced her crying:

> A German woman gives her hand to a French woman, and says in the name of the German delegation that we hope we women can build a bridge from Germany to France and from France to Germany and that in the future we may be able to make good the wrongdoing of men.

Mlle. Mélin replied with an impassioned speech repudiating the statesmen of Versailles and urging the women of the world to unite their forces internationally. An American woman, Emily Green Balch, rose too and raised her hand in a solemn pledge to work with all her power for the abolition of war. Every woman present at the congress stood with raised hand and joined her in this pledge.

Jane Addams, an American delegate, had obtained copies of the official terms of peace on her way through Paris, so the women were able to examine the proposals and make a harshly critical response. The document seemed concerned with dividing the spoils of victory rather than creating a basis for future peace. The Women's Congress criticized the peace terms thus:

> They would create all over Europe discords and animosities which can only lead to future wars. . . . By the financial and economic proposals a hundred million people of this generation in the heart of Europe are condemned to poverty, disease and despair which must result in the spread of hatred and anarchy within each nation.

In particular the women demanded the lifting of the food blockade on Germany and the inclusion of all countries in the League of Nations.

At this conference the Women's International League for Peace and Freedom was formed with headquarters in Geneva. 'Only in freedom is permanent peace possible,' urged Catherine Marshall. Nearly all the delegates had worked for women's freedom—in suffrage and other campaigns—and many had worked for economic and personal freedom for women and men through trade unions and socialist parties. They did not want a peace that depended on oppression. From its foundation WILPF was an international body rather than simply a federation of national sections. Jane Addams was elected President with British and German Vice-Presidents. It was agreed that there could be no peace without the freedom of women to participate in it. A Woman's Charter was proposed which declared 'the recognition of women's service to the world not only as wage earners, but as mothers and home-makers is an essential factor in building up the world's peace.' It also demanded that participating nations should grant equal rights and opportunities to women. Women had a different method of working: 'trying to analyze the meaning of opposing arguments and synthesize the two views, . . . to create agreement and to bring clear expression to all the agreement that is latent among us, . . . all the time trying as much to agree with others as trying to get others to agree with us.'

At the same time, partly because of the suffrage campaign and partly because of the ability that women had shown in the war, British women over thirty were given the vote in 1918 and soon thereafter were also entitled to become MPs.

The international peace movement and the freedom movement were closely related to the new freedoms being discovered in communism and Sylvia Pankhurst played a leading part in setting up the Communist Party in Britain. Catherine Marshall helped to form a Committee for Anglo-Russian Cooperation which organized a mass rally to welcome the revolution at the Albert Hall from which 5,000 had to be turned away because it was full at 12,000. Another suffragist, Helena Swanwick, had reservations and wrote: 'I think no real building can come out of revolutions which make a dust and a mess and bitterness and reaction. They put a premium on violence and spoil thinking and all these industrial questions need very hard thinking.' Since Catherine Marshall was a pacifist it seems likely that she too would have opposed the means of revolution even though she welcomed the new state of society which had emerged in the Soviet Union. Already in 1919 there had been a divergence of opinion in WILPF on the attitude the League should take to the movements of violent revolution in Europe. By only one vote the 1919 Congress resolved that WILPF must maintain its faith in peaceful methods of effecting change, believing that 'it is their special part in this revolutionary age to counsel against violence from any side'.

It was Catherine Marshall who arrived a week before the first Assembly of the League of Nations opened in September 1920 and asked to see the rules of procedure. She was astonished to be told that this was the first time anyone had asked about this. On behalf of WILPF she was concerned about several points such as that the agenda for the Assembly seemed to be decided in advance and that its business was to be conducted in private committees with no minutes recorded. She also pointed out that the people on the Council represented the old order of things and most of them either wanted the League of Nations to do wrong things or to do nothing. WILPF worked in two directions: through its national sections bringing pressure on their governments and through its international office making direct approaches to the delegations. The women saw all too well that nations and their representatives were not transformed by coming to Geneva and participating in the League of Nations. Here there was no lack of chicanery and intrigue and a ceaseless struggle for power. From its foundation WILPF sought for cooperation and insisted that the only effective disarmament was total and universal.

In the early days of WILPF there was considerable pressure on the part of many delegates that the League should become involved in providing relief from the suffering caused by war. However, the decision was taken that the purpose of WILPF was to remove the causes of war rather than to allay the suffering which resulted from it. With its extremely limited resources it had to concentrate its efforts on its special tasks: the study of political and economic issues, objective fact-finding, personal reconciliation, and the formulation of just and humane policies. The Congress in 1924 also considered psychological issues. The need was expressed for a more enlightened system of education and for training in resistance to mass-suggestion. Dr Anita Augspurg pointed out that the most important single factor was 'the bringing into equilibrium of the influence of men and women. Women must cease to admire a man with a gun in his hand and must seek to counteract the destructive tendencies in the masculine mentality by inner devotion to the right'.

During the 1920s WILPF undertook a number of low-key but constructive fact-finding and peacemaking missions in such places as the Balkans, the Rühr, Ireland, Haiti, Indo-China and China. They had also protested against chemical warfare and continued pressure for complete disarmament.

Perhaps the most spectacular demonstration for disarmament was in Britain in 1926. A national 'Peace Pilgrimage' was set up by WILPF with the support of twenty-eight women's and peace organizations under the banner 'Law not War'. Its objects were twofold: to press for a world disarmament conference; and to urge the British Government to sign the Optional Clause of the International Court of Justice to accept compulsory jurisdiction in all disputes of a legal nature. The Peace Pilgrimage set out in May, despite enormous difficulties, along seven main routes to London from the north of Scotland and Land's End, from East Anglia and South Wales. A thousand meetings were held in towns and villages on the way and on June 18th the first contingent entered the outskirts of London. The following day the whole pilgrimage assembled at four rallying points around Hyde Park and from each point a procession set out for the final mass demonstration.

> Here were women of the Guild House in blue cassocks and white collars, bearing their banners aloft; behind them walked members of the League of Nations Union, with bannerettes representing various countries of the world. Here was a carriage filled with women graduates robed in black and scarlet and purple; there was a group of miners' wives. At the head of each procession rode a woman in a Madonna-blue cloak on a white horse.[3]

The speakers were met at Hyde Park by a pageant and on twenty-two platforms speakers from all political parties supported the aims of the demonstration. In 1926 Lucy was still teaching at a school in North Paddington, not far from Hyde Park and may well have been involved in this demonstration.

Meanwhile the WILPF mission to Ireland had produced its report and suggestions, as a result of which the Assistant Secretary of the Irish Labour Party, while admitting that his country could scarcely claim to have an international or pacifist outlook said: 'The Women's International League has come to us with magnificent defiance of the destructive power of hate and a magnificent faith in the power of love informed by intelligence. They have come with that incredible but triumphant declaration that the ideal must become real, that what ought to be will be.'

The League was never content to rest on its lofty ideals but was constantly searching for means of implementing them through constructive action. It frequently found itself in conflict with governmental policies and recognized that its efforts would be of little avail unless governments could be influenced and statesmen approached with human understanding. For this reason the policy was always to work with rather than against government departments and to maintain cordial relations with official representatives, even where strong disagreement over policy occurred.

As the years went by and more countries granted women the vote there was an increasing tendency for women who wanted to influence the policy of world events to seek election to their own governments rather than work through specifically female organizations such as WILPF. Unfortunately in national governments women were in a very small minority and so had little impact. Consequently in this inter-war period, although WILPF continued its work at Geneva, the specifically female voice became muted and military powers and designs again began to grow in Europe.

In September 1930 the women's peace movement was strengthened by the setting up of a Liaison Committee of International Women's Organizations. It comprised the International Alliance of Women, the International Council of Women, the International Federation of University Women, WILPF, the World Union of Women for International Concord and the World YWCA. At the opening of the League of Nations' Eleventh Assembly a delegation went to President Titulescu, with an 'Appeal to the World's Statesmen' on behalf of forty million women in fifty-six countries. A report was made on the manufacture and trade in arms and eight million signatures were collected from women in favour of total disarmament before the first World Disarmament Conference was held in Geneva in February 1932. Already war raged in the Far East, and Europe shivered on the brink of a new catastrophe. It soon became clear that no spectacular progress would be made. The only delegate advocating total disarmament was Litvinoff of the Soviet Union with the support of Turkey. Even the hope of a reduction in arms was thwarted and the Conference ended merely in words.

As the events in Nazi Germany became known WILPF in 1933 expressed its horror at the Nazi crimes and sympathy with the victims. A strong protest against anti-semitism was sent to the German government followed by similar protests from national sections. But in October that year Germany withdrew from the Disarmament Conference, withdrew from the League of Nations and demanded the return of the Saar from France. One other way to peace might still have remained open: the way of economic cooperation long advocated by WILPF. In June 1933 the World Economic Conference took place in London with the participation of sixty-four countries. But this too was doomed to failure. The appeal addressed to all governments by WILPF before the opening of the conference that 'the world's necessity should prevail over nationalistic considerations' fell once again on deaf ears, just as international law had been abandoned in favour of bilateral 'smash-and-grab' agreements. Though this appeal to fundamental reason was to be reiterated for another five years, there was little hope now that, even if listened to, it could have effect in time.

In September 1935 following a brutal wave of anti-semitism in Germany WILPF issued an appeal to non-Jews of Europe that they should not keep silent in face of these crimes. But nothing was done and as Japan, then Italy and finally Germany set out on paths of aggression the members of the League of Nations put national interests before international obligations and so wrecked the first governmental experiment in international cooperation. The abdication of the great powers from the League of Nations and the failure of power politics to offer any alternative system of security led to an upsurge of popular peace movements in the last pre-war years. The peoples of the world were overwhelmingly for peace, but they were fatally divided over the means to its achievement. Consequently the mass peace campaigns made little impact.

At the end of 1937 a British member of WILPF, Muriel Lester, visited China and Japan on behalf of the Fellowship of Reconciliation. On her return she went on a lecture tour of America of which she wrote:

> I shall try to make them see their own share of the guilt. They are making large profits out of supplying the means of death and torture. We women, being practical, must make the public see how ridiculous it is to be angry with people for a crime that would be impossible without our cooperation.

WILPF did not applaud the Peace of Munich but called it a 'sham peace based on the violation of law, justice and right' and declared rather that 'pacifism is *not* quietistic acceptance of betrayal and lies for the sake of "Peace". Pacifism is the struggle for truth, the struggle for right, the struggle for clear political aims, for firm political will and action. Pacifism is courageous initiative for a constructive policy of just peace'. The problem facing the world in 1939 was not so much how to remedy the natural injustices between nations by the exercise of reason and goodwill (which should have been done twenty or thirty years earlier) but how to deal with an aggressive, totalitarian dictatorship without recourse to war.

As the war clouds broke over Europe in December 1939 a small executive committee of WILPF meeting in Geneva made one firm decision for the future, resolving that an International Women's Congress should be held at the time and place of the peace conference which should end the war.

Even during the war the Women's Peace Campaign was active in Britain. There was a Women's Peace Day parade in February 1940 and its seems probable that Lucy took part in this. One of the speakers at a meeting in preparation for it spoke of 'a woman's ability to use her imagination in regarding these terrible events of the war in terms of humanity and not in terms of tonnage and material; the responsibility of womankind for what men are doing now'.

The atomic and then the hydrogen bomb at the end of the war called forth a spontaneous gut reaction from women in numerous protest groups: Women Against the Bomb, Women Oppose the Nuclear Threat, Women's Peace Alliance, The National Assembly of Women and others. Many women joined the ranks of CND. In 1958, the year CND began, there was an all-woman rally, 'Women Against the Bomb' of which Jacquetta Hawkes wrote; 'It could well start a woman's movement against Britain's nuclear armaments at least as powerful as the movement for women's suffrage'. In retrospect, this was probably an understatement.

Canadian women had joined to protest against the nuclear threat in an organization called 'Voice of Women'. In England, Judith Cooke wrote to the *Manchester Guardian* about the dangers from strontium and about the Canadian 'Voice of Women'. There was an immediate response and 'Voice of Women' groups were set up all over Britain. There was also a three-day conference near Cirencester to which Lucy went with a friend from Godalming, staying in a youth hostel overnight.

By the early 1960s there was such a proliferation of women's peace groups that Dorothy Oulton thought it was a waste to have so many different groups all working separately for the same purpose. She suggested amalgamating them into the 'Women's Liaison Committee'. This was done, although many smaller groups were lost along the way. The Liaison Committee had its own news sheet, *Call to Women*, and in the mid 1960s arranged exchanges with women from the USSR through a scheme largely organized by Margaret Curwen called Red Rovers. For many years Lucy, now retired, was treasurer of the WLC and after a long day's work at CND would struggle up to North London for the meeting, arriving with a joke and a smile for everyone.

# 8
# *Retirement*

In 1961 Lucy retired. This meant that she had more time for CND and other peace activities.

By now Mrs Behenna was very unwell and Dorothy gave up her job to nurse her. Their mother died on February 24th, 1962 at the age of 89 and was cremated at Woking on the 28th February, the day on which Lucy would have celebrated her sixty-sixth birthday. Lucy's mother has been described by one of her friends as 'a simple country lady who brought up her family to simple Christian standards in the Victorian style'. She became a member of the Society of Friends only after coming to Godalming where she and her two daughters were the most regular (and sometimes the only) people at meeting. Perhaps the most powerful testimonial to what she was as a person lies in the fact that although Lucy had no children herself she realised that mother-love is one of the strongest forces in the world. It may be significant too, that in a family with no sons, like the Behennas, where the possibility of male competition does not even arise, there is a confidence in the ability of women which is assumed as a natural fact of life.

Soon after their mother died Dorothy sold the house in Tuesley Road and Lucy decided to go and live in Godalming. No doubt the old feeling of responsibility asserted itself and despite appearances to the contrary it seems that the two sisters were very attached to each other. At the same time they both recognized that, although they liked to be near each other, they were incompatible under one roof, so they took neighbouring flats in Filmer Court with windows looking out over the water-meadows. Lucy used to enjoy watching the bird life and especially the herons.

Dorothy now began working as an occupational therapist at the King George V Hospital for tuberculosis patients built among the pine woods about four miles out of Godalming. She was also a pioneer worker with the Old People's Welfare Centre. She was an Elder, Overseer and Clerk of Godalming Meeting.

Lucy was active with the Guldford and Godalming Communist Party, ran a peace stall, in the market, and helped in the Oxfam shop (where they still have vivid memories of her clambering into the window to arrange items for display). She was also learning Russian and following a BBC course on the teaching of literacy.

Lucy was a regular attender at Communist Party meetings and always completely open about it. Her communism was rooted in her deep concern for the poor and a strong determination to ensure that there should never be another war. As one of her Communist friends explained, 'She was totally disinterested in herself. What she believed was how she lived and although she did not aim to go out and convert people, she had her point of view and she stated it firmly. Her life was dedicated to peace.'

During the Vietnam War the Communist Party had a rally outside the library in Guildford. A really militant speaker had just been holding forth with much heckling and hostility and everyone was shouting at him. No-one wanted to speak after this, but Lucy said she would, so she was lifted up on to the rostrum. She could only just see over the edge and had to hang on lest she fall, but she spoke in a very matter-of-fact gentle way about peace, really about peace. She did it her way, not blaming anyone, and the crowd looked absolutely bewildered. They didn't know what to do because she was not talking in the way hecklers love, but quietly and sincerely about peace. And when she had finished she turned and looked at the others, waiting there until they lifted her down off the rostrum.

But her communism could not be accepted by everyone,

and especially not by Dorothy who forbade her to speak at meeting or to become a member. Dorothy would sit on the high level with the Elders, while Lucy sat on the benches below. The crunch came at the time of the Hungarian uprising. One member of the Meeting was so angry about this that she would not go to meeting while a Communist was there. The Elders advised her to go and talk to Lucy about it which she did. From this encounter grew friendship and understanding. Lucy explained how it was her experience of poverty and the cooperation and camaraderie which went with it which had led her to communism, this and the possibility of peace which the early writings of Lenin and others seemed to make a reality. It is doubtful whether she herself ever came to terms with the invasion of Hungary.

Lucy had a large number of Communist text books, many of which she gave to members of the Communist Party when she had to give up her flat. Lucy has underlined parts of the *Communist Manifesto* referring to the exploitation of the working class by the bourgeoisie, but she comments 'Read Belloc's *Servile State* for the twentieth century development of this. New conclusion in light of automation and the A-bomb.' On the back cover of the book Lucy has written 'Belloc in the *Servile State* shows how Capitalism instead of collapsing developed into what he terms the "Servile State" and what was in effect fascism, Nazism and "Churchillism." War greatly helped this development'. She has also marked paragraphs relating to property, but there is no comment beside the paragraphs about women and the family. She no doubt read the books from cover to cover as part of her education as a Communist Party member. But she also read such things as *The Anarchist Red Book* in order to discover how the young were thinking, and derived some amusement from the thought of how scandalized Dorothy would have been by this.

Lucy always remembered the part the Soviet people had played in the war; how they took the brunt of the German aggression up to 1944 and the enormous losses of fighting men and civilians which they suffered, not least in the siege of Leningrad. She would not let it be forgotten that they suffered these terrible losses when fighting in a common cause with the British against the fascism of Nazi Germany, and pointed out that Clementine Churchill at this time was collecting comforts for the Russian front.

Every Friday afternoon the treasurer of the Godalming branch of the Communist Party would call on Lucy at her flat to collect her dues and came to know her well. She perhaps more than any other, was aware of the motherly or grandmotherly aspect of Lucy and recalled her humanitarianism and gentleness which highlighted her beliefs and her sense of humour.

Lucy's sense of humour was recalled by her friend Sylvia Dingwall. In Sylvia's words:

> Lucy said 'Do you see that horse?' There was one solitary horse and it was a bit damp and swampy. It was raining, real April weather, neither cold nor damp but bright. 'You see that horse?' Well it used to be a zebra.' I looked at her thinking 'What do you mean used to be a zebra?' . . . but she looked at me and I looked at her thinking 'Well, it comes to us all some day, . . . something's got to give, . . . shall I just discreetly withdraw from this saying 'Yes, dear, of course it used to be a zebra'? But she looked at me and I looked at her and I thought 'No', so I said 'What do you mean, it used to be a zebra?' and she said 'Well, about ten days ago a circus came to this area you see and they put their horses out to graze in the field and then I saw them come and tether up this zebra. I kept looking out of the window and thinking 'Well, that's the oddest zebra I've seen in my life'. So she got a book out of the library and studied the stripes and the direction of

> the stripes and the width of the stripes and 'Well', she thought, 'This is a very strange species of zebra. Maybe it's very rare.' She kept on looking at it and then she forgot it and got up next morning and had a look again and so on. This went on for days and then it rained. She was watching the zebra and it was raining. And gradually she saw the zebra transforming before her very eyes and the stripes started to dissolve and over a period of about an hour the zebra changed into a horse. So then she realized that its quite difficult to get hold of a zebra and really expensive, . . . but quite easy to get hold of a horse. So the circus people had got hold of a horse and painted it. She was tickled by this. She thought it was wonderful.

One day a week Lucy went to London to work in the CND office which was latterly on the top floor of a house in Great James Street. Climbing the stairs up to this office was itself no mean feat for someone as crippled as she was with arthritis added to the childhood deformity of her legs. The muscles of her leg gave way on two occasions while she was living in Godalming. On one occasion it happened when she was walking on the towpath by the River Wey and she had to be brought home by the police. Even walking to and from the Oxfam shop in Godalming, or the peace stall in the Market Place, or Farncombe station must have been a great effort for one so disabled although she was ready enough to ride pillion on a motorbike even in her seventies when a lift was offered.

It was when she was walking to Farncombe station to go to London for her CND work one morning that she was mugged by a youth who made off with her handbag. Lucy was not concerned about the loss of her handbag (a friend remarked that it probably had nothing in it except paper-clips!) but very concerned about the young man himself. He was brought to trial and put on probation. Lucy found out who he was and went to see him. She discovered that he was illiterate and for this reason could not get a job, so she taught him to read and write.

The careers officer of the Godalming area, Roy Farrant, was becoming very worried during the summer of 1975 about the number of young unemployed in the area. He put a letter in the interdenominational magazine *Link* outlining the possible extent of the problem and the main topics which needed to be considered in tackling it. He offered to be a focal point for ideas and suggestions. Lucy answered this with a letter in which she responded to the appeal with some very practical suggestions on how it might be run and funded. She also suggested a possible venue. No doubt her pre-war experience with the young unemployed people in Willesden was relevant here. One of the main points she made was that the centre should be open to all youth and not just the unemployed so that there should be no segregation (although she pointed out that there were not likely to be any employed people around in working hours). Roy Farrant combined Lucy's ideas with his own and produced a blue-print on which he pencilled in the margin 'based on notes made by Lucy Behenna'. Apparently her encouragement was as important as her suggestions. 'She was a great encourager, with an indomitable spirit. She just would not be put off something that needed doing because of practical difficulties.' At the same time that this plan was produced a young man, Alan Spencer, offered his services and in October a scheme which was to become known as the Witley Enterprises began. After three years, during which seventy youngsters had been helped, it developed into an official scheme run by Waverly Council for the Manpower Services Commission with three centres in Godalming, Farnham and Haslemere. It became a well-established scheme based on a converted pump house in Farnham and it was Alan Spencer, now running his own building business, who came to do the necessary roof repairs.

During the late 1960s and early 1970s support for CND dwindled to a small band of supporters after fears of a nuclear war had been somewhat allayed by the Partial Test Ban Treaty. But throughout this time Lucy continued going up to London every week to work in the CND office. She stayed with them as they moved from Gray's Inn Road, to Bethnal Green, to the top floor of a house in Great James Street. At first she did any work which needed doing, but latterly she was responsible for the bankers' orders. It was often discovered that the bank had made a mistake which had to be chased up and in the course of this work it emerged that the bank had on one occasion mistakenly paid Lucy's pension into Dorothy's bank account. Lucy never told Dorothy about this, perhaps because she thought she would be upset, but perhaps because she felt that this could be some form of compensation for what Dorothy suffered during the war and that if Dorothy realized what had happened she would assume that this was the case. Lucy sold all her surplus furniture in aid of CND and it was with some difficulty that she was dissuaded from giving all her life savings to keep the organization going.

But although she was so generous with her money she would never waste anything. She had a mattress which was going to be thrown away, but having the kind of philosophical attitude that everything has a potential, she took all the feathers out of the mattress and put them in bags and gradually used them to make cushions with a little piping round the edge which she gave to bazaars.

During these years Lucy wanted to plant a Hiroshima tree in Godalming. With some difficulty a Nagasaki cherry tree was found, but then there was a problem about finding a site. Lucy hoped it could be in the Memorial Park, but the

Council would not agree. The vicar suggested the cemetery, but the Church Council refused. Finally a site was found in the garden behind the Friends' Meeting House where two cherry trees now stand beside the boundary wall. Lucy planted the first tree with about a dozen supporters from the Communist Party, CND and the Society of Friends.

# 9
# *Exchange Visits with the Soviet Union*

After their mother died Lucy and Dorothy felt free to travel and during the 1960s, with their friend Joan Castwood, they went by train to Switzerland and then took a coach to Milan, Florence, Rome, Sorrento, Capri, Naples and Genoa. They loved the Yorkshire Dales and went to the York Festival where they saw the Mystery Plays.

Since her first visit to the Soviet Union in 1938 Lucy had been very interested in the country and she was most concerned that the friendship which had existed between the two countries during the war was by the 1960s degenerating into a relationship of fear and hostility. As treasurer of the Women's Liaison Committee she was very supportive of the Red Rover scheme.

In 1962 the Liaison Committee invited women from Russia and from Estonia to come over to England. Four women came in this group and went separately into people's homes. A number of British families in different parts of the country hosted one of these women for a few days at a time and their visit contributed a great deal to mutual understanding. In May 1965 Lucy hosted a research worker in modern English literature from the Ukrainian Academy of Sciences who was the mother of an eleven-year-old daughter. She took her on a tour of London and Guildford, introducing her to the Mayor of Guildford and visiting the cathedral, a woollen factory, a courtroom, a theatre and a secondary school. Reporting on the visit Lucy wrote: 'Everyone was most responsive to the charm of Ena's personality and the combination of scholarship and modesty was often commented on.'

In 1963 Professor Clara Maria Fassbinder organised a pilgrimage of women from many different countries to Rome. This was repeated in 1965 and on that occasion Lucy represented the Liaison Committee. The main theme of this gathering was: 'What women have done for peace and what must still be done.' Some seventy people attended bringing greetings and news from West Germany, France, Spain, Switzerland, Bulgaria, Italy, the USA, the Commonwealth and Britain. Telegrams of support were received from women in the USSR and Poland. The topics introduced and discussed included: 'Psychological Obstacles to Peace' by Professor Fassbinder and 'Catholic Faith and Work for Peace' by the Princess of Ysenburg. Thyssen de Graaf of Holland, a young and gifted graduate, spoke for youth. Lucy reported afterwards:

> We failed in our immediate purpose to be received by the Pope in audience and were disappointed that so few came from Eastern Europe, but the forum was very worth while. As a result of the meeting came the recognition and agreement that the most powerful obstacles to a peaceful world are fear, hunger, ignorance—and greatest of all, Hate. To overcome them we must strive for a more just distribution of this world's goods and, above all, learn to understand and love our neighbour. To me personally comes a deep appreciation of how much our peace work is helped by the freedom of speech and action we enjoy in Britain; denied alas to so many of our continental neighbours.

Every day Lucy spent an hour after lunch learning Russian, but learning languages was never her strong point. She always had great difficulty with French at school and she never became very fluent in Russian although she kept trying.

In 1966 on the Red Rover scheme Lucy went to Russia and Estonia with Joan Scott, Mary Addey and Vera Rice. They set sail from Tilbury on a boat which took five days to reach Leningrad. Here they were met by an interpreter from the Soviet Women's Committee. They visited the Hermitage, then a factory, a kindergarten and a hospital. From Leningrad they went to Tallinn in Estonia where Lucy stayed with one of the women whom she had previously met in England. Otherwise they stayed in hotels, going on from Estonia to Moscow. Lucy sent this description of her visit to *Call to Women:*

> Moscow, for me, had a special interest since I had been there in 1938 when there had been many narrow streets, shabby flats and old wooden houses amidst all the construction work to fulfil 'The Plan'. After the devastation of the war could they possibly have worked on that 'Blue Print' for the future? —They had—the Kremlin and Red Square were as before but now there were many wide tree-lined avenues replacing the narrow lanes and many new blocks of flats, green spaces between them and the necessary nursery, kindergarten and secondary schools, . . . showing that their Socialist plans were being fulfilled. The children are cherished, opportunity is open to all and only peace is needed to fulfil their dreams.[4]

Although she so much respected the achievements of the Soviet Union since the war Lucy was critical of the censorship imposed and the restrictions on reading matter. In many ways too the British women found much in the Soviet Union which seemed to them 'old fashioned'. This did not detract however from the warmth of personal friendship which was created by such visits.

During the 1960s the Red Rover scheme arranged many such exchanges. Although these visits increased understanding and created personal links, the Soviet women were openly dismayed that the British women were so 'ordinary'. The Russian representatives were all lawyers or doctors or professors or high up in their professions. This was partly because they had to speak good English. On the other hand most of the English women going to the Soviet Union spoke little Russian and relied on their hostesses speaking English.

These exchanges finally came to an end for two reasons: the Helsinki Conference and the idea of detente made this sort of exercise seem less valuable if detente was going to happen anyway; and the hostesses were getting tired. The British hostesses were few and always the same. The original idea had been to go to different places each time but this was not really coming about. Nevertheless, although this scheme did not continue it clearly gave Lucy the experience on which she later based Mothers for Peace.

# 10
# *Ifield*

Life became more difficult for the two sisters as they grew older. In 1978 when Lucy was eighty-two they moved into the Quaker housing scheme for the elderly at Ifield Park in Crawley. It had been assumed that they would share a flat there, but again they both opposed the idea, knowing that although they liked to be near each other they could not happily share accommodation.

In one respect it was a sad decision for Lucy because Dorothy insisted that since the Home was run by the Society of Friends and in her belief, communism was incompatible with Quakerism, Lucy must give up her membership of the Communist Party before going to Ifield. This Lucy did, although she continued to belong to the Marxist-Christian dialogue group at Ifield. As she said to a friend, 'labels had become less important'. Lucy herself never had any problem about being both a Quaker and a Communist. Although she told a Communist friend that she did not believe in God in the traditional sense, she believed in 'goodness' and the Christian way of life. In her letters she often said that she was 'waiting for guidance'.

She had applied for membership of the Society of Friends on more than one occasion since her resignation in 1945 but she had always been vetoed by Dorothy and had always accepted this with good grace, leaving the room tactfully before the matter was discussed so that no-one should feel embarrassed. Now at Ifield, having resigned from the Communist Party, she finally became a member of the Society again.

There was also an active CND group in Crawley and Lucy threw herself into this, being elected on to the committee as soon as she arrived. John Cox, who was Chairman of

National CND, also lived in Crawley. In fact she could not have come to a town which was more conscious of peace and nuclear issues. Crawley was a Nuclear Free Zone and for many years had been concerned with peace issues. In 1970, when CND was at its lowest ebb, there was an Easter March from Crawley New Town to Trafalgar Square, partly organized by Crawley Trades Council and headed by the Council's banner. The slogan 'Ban the Bomb—Cut the Arms Bill' aimed to emphasize the adverse effect of arms expenditure on the social services.

Soon after the two sisters arrived at Ifield Dorothy had a stroke. She was completely paralyzed and seemed barely conscious, so had to be moved to a home where she could have more nursing attention. Lucy visited her every day for long hours, making enormous efforts to get through to her, making tape recordings and playing Scrabble or cards with her most evenings. When Dorothy finally died on Good Friday 1979 Lucy was eighty-three. There was a memorial service for her at the Friends Meeting House in Godalming for which Lucy wrote a two-page appreciation of her sister ending with the final tribute: 'A deep sympathy with suffering, an utter devotion to truth were the key motives of a brave spirit.' Dorothy's death was a great sorrow for Lucy but at the same time an enormous release; many people noticed how Lucy seemed to blossom thereafter. The relationship between the two sisters was very complex. When they were still children, Lucy was over-protective of her sister because of her neck deformity, which brought Dorothy into the dominant position. This was reinforced by Lucy's respect for Dorothy's sufferings in the war and the terrible guilt which she always felt for the failure to give her a welcome home. Both sisters were passionately concerned for peace and justice, but whereas Lucy aimed to bring this about through political means by changing the structure of society, Dorothy felt that the change had to come first from within the human being. Dorothy's death not only freed her sister from oppression but also freed her from the resistance to ideas which Lucy, in grieving for her sister, now felt able to absorb. She could now identify with Dorothy's belief in the importance of working through people as well as on a political level. She was also appalled at the cost of Dorothy's funeral and resolved that as she had no family she would not allow her money to be squandered in this way but would put it to good use while she was alive instead.

Meanwhile there was a resurgence of the peace movement. The first signs of CND's revival had appeared during 1973 in Scotland centring on the Polaris submarines. Then there was a growing awareness that the Strategic Arms Limitation Treaty (SALT 1) of 1972 had dangerous limitations which were emphasized by the American move to introduce a 'counterforce' strategy based on a pre-emptive nuclear strike. By the end of the 1970s the neutron bomb appeared and in January 1980 it was revealed that successive British governments had continued with the 'modernization' of the Polaris fleet, called the Chevaline programme, and that the money had been smuggled through the defence budget with only four of the Labour cabinet ministers including Harold Wilson (the Prime Minister), Denis Healey and David Owen knowing about it. This brought a tremendous sense of desolation and despair. Philip Noel-Baker came out of retirement to urge that some action must be taken. It was in fact a time when many of the older generation came to the fore and played a vital part in insisting that new peace initiatives must be found. It started Lucy thinking on the lines which led to Mothers for Peace and it brought a tremendous revival of CND.

Part of this revival was the formation of a CND group in Godalming; Lucy went to the inaugural meeting. A God-

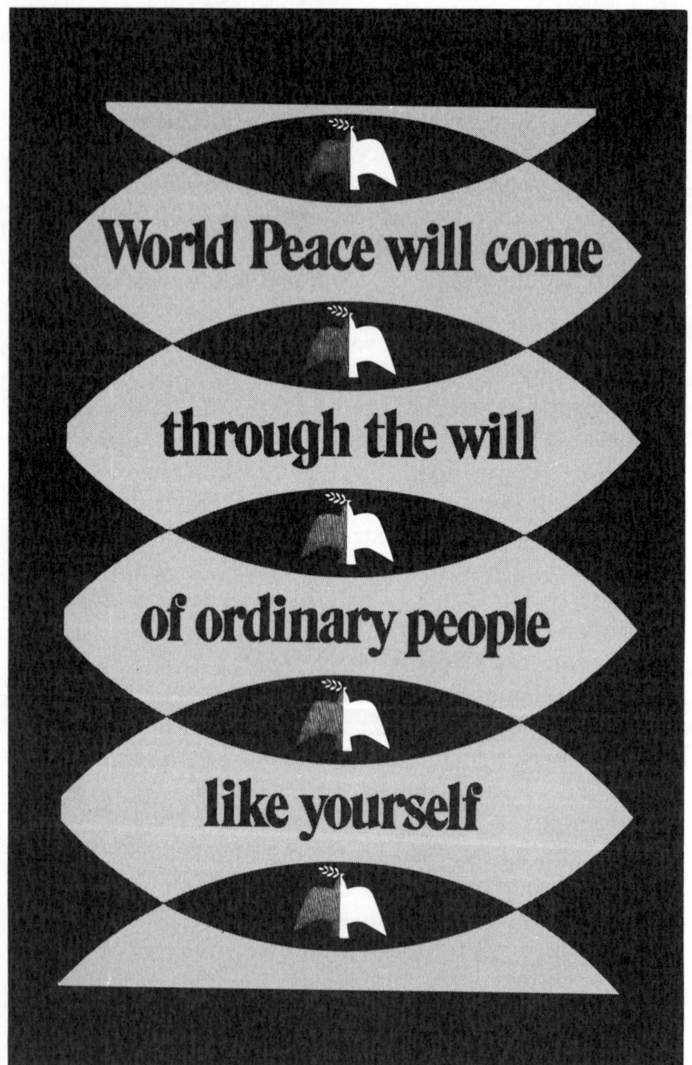
World Peace will come
through the will
of ordinary people
like yourself

A QPS poster

alming friend was surprised to see Lucy walking up the hill towards the meeting place having come over by train. Lucy sat on the front row and spoke passionately, not least in reminding the audience of the fact that the Soviet Union had been our ally in the last war. Unfortunately she was too polite to turn her back on the people sitting at the front table so she spoke with her back to the audience and much of what she said could not be heard.

However, CND was entirely a matter of protest and Lucy must have realized that protest was not enough. Realistically no nation would give up its nuclear weapons or any other weapons unilaterally unless there was a strong alternative network of trust and cooperation. Only in such a situation would arms become irrelevant. She realized that mothers were in a position to create this cooperation and trust. She told how one day she saw a poster saying 'World Peace will come through the will of ordinary people like yourself'.She remembered her children in the East End shelter and ideas began to germinate.

# 11
# *A New Initiative: Mothers for Peace*

The time was ripe for a new peace initiative. Dorothy's death had given Lucy a new freedom but more critical was that Lucy met a friend at Ifield whom she had known some years before: a fellow teacher and kindred spirit who was able to help Lucy translate her ideas into action. This was Marion Mansergh.

Both Marion and Lucy had been teachers and had never married. Whereas Lucy was small and crippled Marion was tall and with an exceptionally fresh and young complexion. Mansergh is a Westmoreland name but Marion, like Lucy, was born in London, where her father was an architect. Her father had an accident while at school, falling on his head in the gymnasium. It was thought that this was the cause of a brain tumour from which he died at the age of forty-two. After his death Marion went back with her mother and older brother to live in Southampton, which was her mother's home. When Marion first left school she did not know what she wanted to do and for a while worked in the Ordnance Survey office. But when she was twenty she decided she wanted to be a teacher and trained for three years at the Southampton teacher training college on the University College campus. On leaving college, she taught in a mixed school for boys and girls.

When the war came in 1939 Marion was evacuated to Church Knowle near Corfe Castle. A billet had been arranged for her but when she arrived it had been taken by someone else, so the man who was driving her said 'Let's see what my Mum can do' and took her to his home, where an attic was found for her on the top floor above 'Ye Olde

Tea Shoppe'. Here she lived for three years. The school house in Corfe Castle had been closed for many years but it was opened at the time Marion arrived to provide education for evacuees from London. 'And very tough they were too,' Marion commented. For two weeks she had two dozen children with no equipment except a piano.

Marion was not a Quaker by birth. While she was studying the different denominations at training college a visit was arranged to a Friends Meeting. Later, when she was on holiday with another teacher, they wanted to go to Sunday morning worship. She was Anglican and her friend was Methodist so they decided to compromise by going to a Quaker meeting again. From that time on she attended on a fairly regular basis and became a member of the Society of Friends in 1948.

After teaching for some years Marion got very impatient with what she called 'the X,Y,Zs.' So she decided to give them special attention. She took a course with the Central Association of Mental Welfare, after which she always taught remedial classes, except during the war.

Marion first met Lucy when she came to Dorking and Horsham Monthly Meeting from Godalming. They met again when both were residents at Ifield. Here Marion's main interest was in supporting Amnesty International. It seems that Marion laid the foundations on which Lucy's charisma could flourish. Lucy had the energy and loved public speaking whereas Marion abhorred publicity but had the brains and the direction. It was certainly a creative combination.

Lucy had a small L-shaped room not far from the dining room at Ifield. A french door opened onto the corner of a stone patio. Marion used to visit her most evenings before the evening meal and one day Lucy remarked: 'I'm going to put some money aside so that mothers here can go and meet Russian mothers.' Marion said 'Well, I will too.' When she later discovered all the publicity in which she would be involved, she says, she almost regretted it.

Lucy worked out that in sheltered housing she wouldn't need much. She didn't plan to spend a great deal on clothes or holidays so she would put a little aside for her funeral and could then live on her pension. This meant she could give all the rest of her savings, a thousand pounds, to the project. Marion realized that she could do the same. This was at the beginning of 1980 when, with the new awareness of the nuclear threat, all sorts of ideas were flying around. Grace Crookall-Greening in the Quaker Peace & Service department at Friends House remembers receiving a letter from Lucy at this time sparsely written on one side of a piece of blue paper suggesting that mothers should band together for peace. This was not taken very seriously because Lucy was just a little old lady who was not a mother herself and there were so many other ideas being suggested. However, Lucy persisted and after a meeting at Ifield where Gerald Trent (Lucy's argumentative colleague in CND) had spoken strongly in support of Philip Noel-Baker, and Grace herself had spoken on the same theme, Lucy came along to Grace afterwards to urge her idea again. She wrote to the local papers. Friends began to listen to her and take her idea seriously.

At the end of June 1980 the Quaker weekly journal *The Friend* contained the following verse by Edith Simpson entitled 'The Tinder Box':

We sit in our meeting for worship
In silence, enveloping, deep;
Eyes downcast (to any unknowing
It might seem that we were asleep;)
Some of us seem grey-haired or balding,
All quiet in clothing and speech;
Yet here fused in thought, we are tinder
That lighted the whole world can reach

And turn from its course of destruction,
Revealed in that powerful flame—
O God come among us,ignite us
And send us abroad in Thy name.[5]

On August 1st in the same magazine a letter from Lucy appeared headed 'A Mission to Mothers'. She wrote:

In *The Friend* of June 27th appeared a poem which ended:

. . . ignite us
And send us abroad in Thy name.'

Since then I have talked with some Friends and other friends and they think the following idea is worthy of consideration. This would be to get together a group of concerned mothers who would go to the Soviet Union with a message of goodwill to Russian mothers.

They would assure them that we have neither wish nor will to kill or mutilate their children, and we are sure they don't wish to harm ours. Love for our children, and the desire to give them a happy childhood and a future is the link between us.

We would say that we know that their government is working for disarmament to make this possible; and that we are working to encourage our government in its efforts to the same end.

Could you give this idea publicity and so test out, by response, if it is just a 'notion' or a 'genuine spark'?[6]

This letter had a most encouraging response. Lucy then obtained the approval of Ifield Preparative Meeting for her proposal and they sent it on to Dorking and Horsham Monthly Meeting who invited Lucy to come and tell them about it. So at the next Monthly Meeting she shared her concern to organize a mission of mothers to the Soviet Union and the United States. She suggested that such a mission of mothers to mothers, all with a mutual hope for peace, might encourage the governments to seek to realize their stated aims with more persistence and enthusiasm.

The members of this Meeting supported Lucy and recommended that she should be given the opportunity of speaking about her project to the Society's executive body, Meeting for Sufferings, at Friends House in London, at which representatives came from all over the country. So on November 1st 1980 Lucy and Marion attended Meeting for Sufferings at Friends House.

The Meeting began with an account of a visit to Jamaica and then followed the Accounts and Estimates for the year. There was a description of a 'Project for Partnership' among black and white churches, followed by an analysis and response to the British White Paper on the Nationality Law. Last of all came Lucy. She spoke from below the dais and someone who was present recalled what a sincere thrill she experienced in hearing 'that little old lady put her whole heart and soul into the exposition of her thoughtful and exciting concern'. She described it more fully in these words:

> The next to last item on the agenda on that Saturday was introduced by a very tall young man, with the microphone at the appropriate level, and he was followed in striking contrast by this little old lady, for whom the microphone had to drop to its lowest point. But her vivacity and enthusiasm made her for me the most inspiring speaker.

*The Friend* recorded:

> Lucy explained how she had first shared her ideas to try and organize a mission of mothers to the Soviet Union and the US with readers of *The Friend* last August. The first inkling of it had occurred when she read the words of a Quaker Peace & Service poster: 'World Peace will come through the will of ordinary people like yourself'. It seemed to her that some new initiative for peace was needed. It was only later that she connected mothers

and peace. Why? Because mothers the world over had a common bond. They all loved their children and had extra love to spare. 'Therefore if mothers in this world could get together, something might happen', reasoned Lucy Behenna . . .

It was with evident glee that Lucy Behenna went on to recount how the developments gathered momentum. She recalled how she was being interviewed by the editor of the local paper on an entirely different matter. At the end of the interview he said rather sarcastically, 'Well Miss Behenna, and have you any other good ideas?' 'Indeed I have,' I replied. 'No young mother in this country or any other wants her son to go and kill the sons of other young mothers and I believe that if inter-visitations were arranged between parties of young mothers from Britain, the USA and Russia and from other countries who chose to join in, bridges of under-standing could be built between countries who know little of each other as a REAL contribution to world peace.' The editor was impressed and publicized the idea in his paper, illustrating it with a photograph of the 'two pensioners' who had sparked it off. It aroused great interest. Then Lucy Behenna talked about it on the radio and ITV referred to it. The result had been money and letters in support and definite arrangements were now being made for a small number of young mothers to go as a group both to the United States and the Soviet Union on a peace mission, if possible early next year. (Lucy Behenna made it quite clear that neither she nor her friend had it in mind to join them.) Already organ-izations in both countries had indicated that such visits would be welcome, and offers had been received by a number of mothers, including one with a knowledge of Russian, willing to undertake the journey.

The Meeting responded warmly to the concern Lucy

> Behenna laid before them and in addition to encouraging her and Marion Mansergh to carry it forward, it asked Quaker Peace & Service, which was already fully in the picture, to help them in any way that seemed appropriate.[7]

Mothers for Peace was launched.

# 12
# *The First Stages*

So, with the blessing of the Society of Friends and £2,000 in the kitty, Lucy set off on her pensioner's rail card to speak about her idea in various parts of the country and raise the necessary money and support to make her dream come true. At this time British Rail were offering £1 rail cards to pensioners for unlimited travel during November.

Lucy's faith and determination somewhat exceeded her competence when it came to rail travel. Her hostesses discovered that she would almost certainly not arrive on the train they expected and probably not even from the direction anticipated. This was rather disconcerting for those meeting her at the station, but she always found someone to help her with a lift in a car or even by lifting her bodily out of the train.

In November Lucy visited the national CND Conference in Leeds where Bruce Kent gave her publicity and she was encouraged to hear two items of news which she passed on to her audiences in later meetings. The first of these items was that a group of high-ranking Dutch military officers were considering asking their government to 'declare the use of nuclear weapons a war-crime' and the second that a senator who had previously been a high-ranking general in NATO was now devoting all his energies to working for disarmament. Lucy found great encouragement also in Lord Louis Mountbatten's stand against nuclear weapons and frequently referred to this in her speeches.

With the help of Rowland Dale, Secretary of the Northern Friends Peace Board, and 'a terrifying number of telephone calls', she visited Sheffield, Manchester, Glasgow, Edinburgh and Carlisle. At every town hospitality had been arranged and she spoke at public meetings, went on radio and had a 'write-up' in the local press. *The Guardian* too gave the Mothers for Peace a paragraph.

By 25th November Lucy was up in Scotland, where she was interviewed by Frances Horsburgh on BBC Scotland. Frances asked her about the thinking behind the mothers' trip, to which Lucy replied: 'Mother love is one of the greatest powers and it is universal. Mothers of all creeds and colours, religions and no religions at all, whatever government they are under, desire the best for their children and I thought that great link between mothers we might use to help break down a little of the fear and mistrust, so I thought of a group of mothers going to America and a group of mothers going to the USSR with this message.'

On being asked what kind of reception she thought they would get, Lucy stated: 'The reception they have already got is that the Soviet Women's Peace Committee have sent us a cordial acceptance of our wish to go and are arranging meetings for us in Moscow, Leningrad and Kiev. The Women's League for Peace and Freedom, which is the big American peace organization, have offered us hospitality. If we once get to New York we shall have no further troubles and they are also arranging meetings so that we are assured of meeting the mothers of both countries if we get there – and I'm sure we shall get there.

'So the final aim is world disarmament,' Frances Horsburgh commented. 'What kind of impact do you think young mothers can make on that aim?

'The first impact they'll have is on the sons and husbands of the other side. Sons and husbands, especially if they have good mothers and are happy with their wives, will listen and some of them no doubt will be delegates who will go to the special disarmament commission in 1982. They will go with a different attitude. They will go this time thinking, we MUST get a practical measure taken because of Tom and Dick and Betty. We can't go back and say "We've only suggested we might possibly do something." They must go back saying "We have agreed to do the first step towards disarmament".

'You are eighty-four years old yourself,' the interviewer pointed out, 'and you have been working for peace almost all your life. Are you still optimistic that we'll ever see a world without nuclear weapons?'

'Well, I'm optimistic to this extent,' Lucy replied. 'I believe there is a power greater than ourself which shapes our ends, rough hew them how we will, and I firmly believe that if we do our share and we don't think we can have it cheaply, without effort, without putting our efforts and our money into it, that this can be halted. Nuclear weapons and nuclear war is under man's control. It is not a flood, or a plague, or a volcanic eruption. And if those of us who want to give our children their lives work hard enough and don't expect to get it on the cheap without work or cash, I do believe the arms race can be halted, even at this late hour.'

Lucy often referred to 'our children', no doubt thinking of the children she had taught and the children she might have had and, especially those children in the East End shelter waiting for the buzz bomb to drop, which she mentioned so many times on her campaign tour. She had instinctively tapped into the most powerful peacemaking power in the world. Whereas the early women's peace movement had been founded on the common desire of women in many countries for suffrage, a preliminary goal which enabled women to work together for far more fundamental issues of peace and freedom, Lucy had now emphasized the deepest possible common denominator between women of all nations, which could provide the power and energy to achieve their universal aims for a future where the children of all the world could live and grow in cooperation, security and hope.

But Lucy's vision was always grounded on a practical basis. She would relate how she and Marion had been able to donate £1,000 each from their savings to start the fund for Mothers for Peace and how another thousand had been donated by friends. When she finished her talk she would say frankly: 'If you'd like to help with a donation, we shall very gratefully receive it.' It was not long before she had the necessary £5,000 in donations of from £1 to £200.

Apart from gaining the support of Quakers, Lucy also obtained, by December, the backing of the World Disarmament Campaign, the Women's International League for Peace and Freedom, the Cooperative Women's Guilds and the Liaison Committee of Women's Peace Groups.

Marion Thorpe remembers Lucy coming to a meeting of the Liaison Committee and saying: 'Do you think I am mad?' with a twinkle in her eye. They thought that she was optimistic, but she was so obviously inspired that they gave her their support.

Lucy wrote to Freddy Laker to ask if he would provide cheap flights for the mothers but these were not forthcoming. Nevertheless, by January 1981, Lucy had booked two flights, one to New York and one to Moscow, both leaving Gatwick on May 2nd. It took the Travelcare agent in Crawley almost two hours to achieve this near miracle of two flights from the same airport on the same date, for which she recorded her sense of gratitude. She then got to work with visas and passports and was already thinking ahead to the speaking tours which the mothers would make on their return in which they would tell the public about their mission.

The Liaison Committee for Women's Peace Groups asked in its newsletter that readers should send the delegates letters of support so that each delegate could take with her hundreds of these letters signed by as many people as possible.

There was a suggested form of words for explaining what those signing would be supporting:

> Feeling that governments have failed to implement the declared aim of the nations of the world expressed in the UN, which called for general and complete disarmament, and that ordinary people can exert pressure and so help to bring this about:
>
> Young British mothers representing many peace groups wish to initiate peaceful relations with young mothers in the USA and the USSR thus making a three-way link which can bypass diplomatic channels and break the barrier of a fear which is one of the factors preventing disarmament. It is hoped to maintain this three-way communication on peace issues so that we will never arrive at a point where our children will fear a future war.

Members were asked to collect signatures from peace groups, church people, specially selected celebrities and people belonging to no special group or organization. It was pointed out that the childless too could sign because 'our' children must mean the children of our country.

The World Disarmament Campaign also described the project to the readers of its newsletter, urging them to obtain signatures and help with publicity.

Lucy urged everyone to collect signatures and to work inside their groups to help build the peace movement into a mighty force. 'We must get action. We will if we work hard enough. We have just a year before the UN Special Session on Disarmament. Thus the aim of us all will be a happy childhood and a worthwhile future for children everywhere.'

In less than a year from its inception the scheme was in action.

# 13
# *Selection of Mothers*

Having raised the money, Lucy and Marion now needed to select the applicants. They wanted mothers with young children who had some kind of relevant qualification and who had been active in the peace movement: four to go to the Soviet Union and four to the USA.

Margaret Cooper was chosen as the leader of the Russian group. She was a nurse who had worked her way twice round the world before getting married and in the process learned to pilot a plane. She worked in an Oxfam shop, was a member of CND and, above all, spoke Russian. Margaret explained her commitment to Mothers for Peace in these words: 'Women are the creators and nurturers of life and it is our children, our sons and daughters who are going to be the next people to be involved in war. Surely in the long term it is easier to disarm friends than to disarm an enemy.' She pointed out that the display of military might in Red Square parades was the outcome of deep fear and insecurity, for Russia had been invaded again and again. She wanted to play a part in developing a more permanent and lasting friendship. The others selected to go with her to the Soviet Union were Jenny Hartland, Wendy Franklin and Jill McMinn.

Sheila Ragg, who led the American group, was a social worker and a lecturer on third world subjects. For her the crunch had come when it was realized that British bases were being used for cruise missiles. 'We suddenly became aware that we had our heads buried in the sand', she said. 'Europe awoke from a long sleep to find the threat right on our doorstep.' The three mothers who went with Sheila to the USA were Pat Dale, Shenagh Gleisner and Rilba Jones.

Lucy arranged the tickets and the visas and the eight

mothers met several times in London to get to know each other. On the evening before their departure, they all met in Crawley.

Although Lucy had lived in Crawley for only a few years she was a highly respected and much loved member of the peace movement there. She was given great local support with this project. On the evening before departure there was a dinner at the Grange Hotel in Crawley to wish the mothers 'God speed'. Representatives were present from most of the supporting organizations. Lucy and Marion were given flowers. Together they all read the International Prayer for Peace:

Lead me from Death to Life, from Falsehood to Truth.
Lead me from Despair to Hope, from Fear to Trust.
Lead me from Hate to Love, from War to Peace,
Let Peace fill our Hearts, our World, our Universe.

On the morning of May 2nd eight mothers flew off from Gatwick airport, four going east to the Soviet Union and four west to the United States all bearing the good wishes of thousands of people represented by a small crowd of well-wishers including Lucy, Marion and the Crawley Peace Group. With them they carried the message:

> We British mothers do not wish to harm your children, nor do we believe you wish to harm ours. The link between us is love of our children and the desire to give them a happy childhood and a secure future. This can only be done if disarmament—first nuclear and then general—takes place. We must break down the barrier of fear between us, which is one of the factors preventing disarmament, and work together to persuade our governments to halt the arms race and then to disarm. We thank you for your peace work to date and wish you well. Yours in friendship—Mothers of Britain.

They also took with them copies of a peace poster quot-

Marion Mansergh (right) and Lucy (left), 85 years old, at Gatwick Airport prior to the departure of Mothers for Peace to the USSR in 1981. *QPS picture collection.*

ing the words of Lord Louis Mountbatten pointing out the futility and insanity of a nuclear arms race.

While they were away the Society of Friends held them in a rota of prayerful support which meant that someone was thinking of them every hour during their absence. This was a source of strength and gave the visits spiritual depth as Lucy later pointed out in her introduction to the account of these visits.

# 14
# *Mothers in the Soviet Union, 1981*

Margaret, Jenny, Jill and Wendy arrived in Moscow late in the evening of May 2nd and were greeted with a friendly smile from the customs official who obviously approved of them. Moscow was still draped with May Day banners, many of which bore peace messages. Purple lilac trees were in bloom all over Moscow and many people were carrying flowers.

On the first morning, the group visited Red Square which was crowded with many families out enjoying the sights and the warm spring weather. One of the mothers recalled that 'We deliberately kept reminding one another that these people, the old women, the children pulling little wooden toys on wheels, were supposed to be our enemies. We failed completely to make the connection.'

During the afternoon two very dignified members of the Soviet Women's Committee visited them in their hotel and talked for several hours, covering many subjects from peace work in England to the general day-to-day lives of women in both countries. One of these women, Ludmilla, had known Lucy from her visit in 1968. They pointed out that there had been little contact between English and Russian groups during the last ten or fifteen years although there had been exchanges with other countries. Their concern for peace and international understanding was mutual. Both Soviet women had travelled quite a distance to meet the English mothers and on a public holiday as well.

On the following morning they met the Secretary of the Soviet Peace Committee and had a long talk. They came away feeling convinced that this widely respected body afforded a genuine vehicle for public opinion, and that the ultimate aim of total disarmament was shared.

Later on they were interviewed by Georg Murzin of the Moscow Radio World Service. Already the mothers were realizing that they should not think of themselves as a 'mission' because Soviet people were already committed to peace and had at least as much experience of organized peace campaigning as anyone in the West. They also came to realize that their own experience of war was peripheral compared with the terrible suffering of mothers in the Soviet Union whose country had been invaded five times in the last two centuries with a human loss of millions. This understanding was reinforced by visiting the war cemeteries in Leningrad and Kiev where the scale of loss and the grief for so many dead was still a very present reality. There were fresh flowers on all the war graves and the tomb of the unknown soldier was guarded by Young Pioneers who obviously felt it a great honour. The mothers commented that they had seldom seen so many adults so visibly moved and openly grieving. Yet they sensed no lingering bitterness against Germany, only a determination that history would never be repeated. While they were there, young brides were bringing their bouquets to lay on the graves as a pledge that they would remind their children of the sacrifices which had been made by an earlier generation. To some of the English visitors it was an almost overpoweringly tragic experience. The bus returning from the Leningrad cemetery was like a tomb. No-one spoke. Even five years later, Margaret said she had a headache at the mere thought of the cemetery. It was like a block of concrete coming down into her mind. Yet the Russians remembered their alliance with England in the war.

On Monday evening the mothers flew to Kiev, capital of the Ukraine. They made a tour of the city in the morning, seeing why it was aptly called 'The Green City', with many parks and broad streets lined with horse-chestnut trees. They saw with delight the red squirrels, nesting boxes put in the trees for birds, and countless lines of benches under the trees for the benefit of the people. Many grandmothers were taking babies for a walk while their mothers were at work.

One of the most memorable visits of the tour took place on the Wednesday morning when the mothers went to the offices of the Ukrainian Soviet women's magazine. The mothers sat at one end of a small room and the rest of the staff all tried to squeeze in, even standing on the window sills. Most of them did not speak English, but there was a red-haired interpreter from the Ukrainian women's peace group. Sitting opposite Margaret, foursquare, with her hands resting on her knees was a massive woman who must have weighed about eighteen stone. She wore naval uniform with gold bars across the sleeves and was loaded with medals. She had been a sea-captain with her own ship in the last war and was now in her seventies (although she did not look it) and was at that time a professor in some branch of naval architecture. She was also a mother and had the Order of Lenin. She had jet black hair and intense concentration in her eyes which never wavered as she listened to them. At first she sat gazing stolidly at them with a mask-like expression, but gradually, as the English mothers spoke, her face transformed in sheer delight. Finally she herself gave an impassioned speech in Russian about her wartime experiences and her yearning for peace, driving her points home with almighty thumps of her fist. The mothers explained about the diversity of peace groups in England which the Russians found hard to understand, although they were impressed that these were young mothers who had come rather than retired women, and also that they had come without official sponsorship. They were intensely surprised to hear about Lucy's letter and a fruitful discussion followed. In the centre of the table was a samovar and many truffle-like cakes which were dispensed and then each of the mothers was given a piece of pottery. The meeting ended with hugs all round and an overwhelming feeling of like-mindedness.

While in Kiev the group also visited a school, were interviewed for Radio Ukraine and spent the evening with the Ukrainian Friendship Society. They were impressed by the standard of English in the schools and by the high proportion of the national budget which seemed to be spent on children, who were regarded as 'a most precious and somewhat scarce commodity'. Before leaving they found the 'Children's World', a whole traffic-free street of children's shops selling clothes, books, toys, writing and painting materials, all beautifully made and inexpensive.

As they went north the birch forests gave way to tundra marshes and became yellower and yellower as mushy snow retreated. When they stepped out of the train in Leningrad the cold hit them. It was freezing. Here again as they drove from the airport they were impressed by the sheer grinding hard work of rebuilding after the war.

Once more they heard harrowing first-hand experiences of the war from women who had watched their husbands and children starve to death. That particular week in May is crowded with celebration in the USSR. It begins with May 1st and ends with Victory Day on the 9th—the day of liberation in 1945. The meetings were all set against this background and the mothers appreciated the time that was found for them, realizing that it was a very good week for focusing on the problems of war and the search for peace. On Saturday evening they visited an Orthodox Church. The usual service was in progress with beautifully accompanied singing. There were many people there of all ages, including babes in arms. Outside the church an old man stood by his son's grave telling a group of about twenty people of his wartime loss. There was no bitterness, only a great sadness.

Margaret returned with many memories; in particular she remembered the woman at Friendship House who had described her experience in the Leningrad blockade. The food began to run out and thousands starved to death. Her husband was not well enough for military service so lived with her and her baby in a little flat. She was quite young then. They had a piece of bread about the size of a matchbox each day and melted snow for water. Her husband refused to eat and gave his bread to the child. He died first. A few weeks later the little boy died. She had to take their bodies outside and leave them to be collected by sledges which took them to collecting centres and in the spring, when the ground unfroze, they were bulldozed into the earth. She has no idea where they are buried. When she met the mothers from England she said 'You cannot believe how happy I am you are here. I see you as a hope for our country and for the world'. Another woman, when they said 'goodbye' impulsively came back and, tearing the amber beads from her neck, put them on Margaret.

It was an exhausting week but packed full of experiences and encounters which would provide material for speaking engagements every weekend for the next year as new understanding and hope was brought to ever wider circles.

# 15
# *Mothers in the USA, 1981*

Meanwhile Sheila, Pat, Shenagh and Rilba were in America, a country which has not known war on its own soil for well over a hundred years. This was immediately highlighted in the marked contrast between the achievement of the country and its capacity for aggression and destruction as revealed in the Air and Space Museum which the mothers visited in Washington. Here hordes of patriotic schoolboys clambered into space ships, or eagerly inspected the lunar module of the US moon landing. But close at hand, towering through two storeys, dwarfing the nearby staircase and the people, stood some missiles, including Minuteman III with a nuclear capacity fourteen times that of the Hiroshima bomb in each of fifteen warheads. In the next gallery was the shell of 'Little Boy', subsequently recovered from the debris of Hiroshima, with a brief account beside it of the dangers of atomic warfare; but it looked like a museum piece and to the fervently patriotic little boys it had none of the glamour of space-craft. The mothers noted that the unemotive inscription conveyed neither the horror of the first atomic bomb nor the consequences for Hiroshima. There was, however, a reminder of the cooperation which had been achieved between Russia and America in the Apollo-Soyuz linked space-craft.

The mothers found many sincere and dedicated people who felt just the way they did, but among the ordinary people whom they met in the streets, in the shops, and on public transport, there emerged from their initial warmth and friendliness a hostile response to the Soviet Union, a distrust and deep suspicion of it, which sprang from an often unshakeable belief in the military supremacy of

Mothers for Peace in USA in 1981: left to right: Rilba Jones, Shenagh Gleisner, Sheila Ragg and Pat Dale. *QPS picture collection.*

Russia, particularly in the field of nuclear technology. They noticed that conversations which began warmly and expressed an interest in Britain suddenly cooled when they explained the purpose of their visit. Almost everyone seemed to support Reagan's defence budget (which meant that defence would account for one-third of all government spending in five years' time) and wanted a strong president to make the United States strong again. Some were surprised that they should visit the United States on such a mission (and they were glad to be able to talk about their counterparts in the Soviet Union) while others felt they were ungrateful because the United States had saved Britain during the world wars. The mothers were tremendously impressed by the helpfulness and the courtesy of Americans wherever they went and yet on the subject of 'defence' or 'disarmament' they seemed to be quite different people.

They stayed at Davis House, the international Quaker hostel in Washington, and Quakers arranged a programme of visits and meetings so that they might both gather information and give it. Usually in pairs, they talked to church groups and women's groups and students. Their message was clear: the only way to a safe future for their children was disarmament; they emphasized the folly of civil defence plans as set out in the British government booklet *Protect and Survive*[8] and the colossal waste of money and resources on arms while fifteen million children die annually of malnutrition.

Reactions varied from an inability even to contemplate nuclear war because it was 'unthinkable' to an unwavering desire for increased armaments and a strong defence as a protection against Soviet aggression. Even young people at the Friends School, whom they expected might yearn for a secure future, on the whole felt more threatened by the Soviet Union and possible invasion with the ultimate threat of communism, than by the fragile and unstable balance of nuclear technology which meant that a computer error could destroy both civilization as we know it and possibly all life in the northern hemisphere. They were often asked whether they would rather be red than dead.

The mothers were able to give a great deal of information both to meetings and to peace organizations about the movement in Britain and throughout Europe. Many Americans knew nothing about the proposed development of cruise missiles, nor even that the US bases existed in Britain. They were surprised at the ignorance about European anti-war movements as well as taken aback at the vehement assertions that the Soviet Union was well ahead of the United States in military technology and weaponry. They appeared on the Fred Fisk Show with Laura Hepner of the Women's Party for Survival and talked about the Mothers for Peace project, their work for peace in Britain, the European peace movement, the numbers, sophistication and expense of nuclear weapons, the uselessness of civil defence, alternatives to defence industries such as the Lucas Aerospace Corporate plan and even alternative forms of defence such as nonviolent resistance.

They had a lengthy interview with a young woman reporter from the *Washington Post* in which they spoke of their fears for their children, the need for disarmament, and their surprise at the strength of anti-Soviet feeling, telling of the Russians they had met, who spoke of their people's desire for peace. Unfortunately, the report was slanted to present them as naive and 'left-wing'. However an ex-military man wrote to the paper in their support, pointing out that the naive people were those who thought that to have peace you must prepare for war.

Despite encountering so much hostility to their message, they did meet some peace organizations and were able to arrange a showing of Jonathan Dimbleby's film *The Bomb*. They also met Zelle Andrews, the first full-time peace worker of the United Church for Christ, and attended a briefing session for congressmen by Scientists Against Nuclear Extermination on the development of cruise missiles. They were also able to attend the final session of the Peace Churches Seminar where Paul Warnke, the chief US negotiator at the Salt II talks, was speaking and exchange views and experiences with the delegates from all over the States.

Having been encouraged by the response to a petition, 'Call a Halt to the Arms Race', calling for a bilateral freeze on armaments, which was supported by 59 to 41% out of 33 districts carrying for Reagan, Shenagh and Sheila balanced the picture by going along to the Veterans of Foreign Wars, an extreme right wing body which enjoys tremendous prestige and great influence on the government. The veterans talked of their belief in a 'clean' neutron bomb, which would kill people rather than destroying buildings and blamed the Russians for being the first to develop small tactical nuclear weapons. Little dialogue was possible in this situation.

After a week Shenagh and Rilba flew home while Pat and Sheila stayed for two more days to share in the Mothers' Day March and Rally for Disarmament. Unfortunately it was a wet day and the turn-out was relatively small, but Sheila and Pat walked from the Capitol to the White House with Americans, and particularly mothers, concerned for the future of their children and humankind. Babies kept dry in prams while passing motorists hooted in support. There were many moving speakers at the rally, including Helen Caldicott, author of *Nuclear Madness*[9] and founder of the Women's Party for Survival, who spoke as a mother of her concern for children whatever their race, nationality or creed. The British mothers were able to deliver their own message of peace and friendship and to emphasize the unwillingness of Europe to be a battlefield for the two super-powers. The following morning they joined mothers on the steps of the Capitol for a rally before the Americans went to lobby congressmen and the British flew home. The same fears and anxieties that mothers in Britain felt for their children and for civilization were expressed by mothers from all parts of the United States. They felt a strong affinity and a sense of hope that ordinary people could influence governments if they were sufficiently motivated. They came away knowing that the lasting memory would be of friendships made; the parting with Laura Hepner on the Capitol steps, when they embraced in the rain on that last morning, represented the desire for peace and friendship which crosses oceans and national boundaries.

# 16
# *Return Visit*

Lucy and Marion met the peace passengers (as they sometimes called them) when they returned to Gatwick. A programme of meetings was now arranged for the mothers to go round the country telling of their experiences. Usually they went in twos, one from the American tour and one from the Soviet tour.

Lucy had given them pocket money to spend while they were away but there was still quite a lot left when they returned. This was put towards a return visit of Russian and American mothers the following summer.

It was a warm spring day in 1982, when London was at its greenest, that a party of nine American and six Soviet mothers were welcomed by the British Mothers for Peace. That evening there was a meeting at the Penn Club. One of the young Russian mothers, Maria, vividly remembers that day. The Soviet women arrived after the Americans who, they sensed, were tense and apprehensive (as they later admitted they had been). But Lucy was absolutely sure of it. She approached Maria, as the youngest Russian there, and introduced her to the youngest American mother. Maria recalls Lucy as a very frail old lady, but very outgoing and determined that everyone should be friends, clearly showing her delight when she saw that conversation was developing and that they liked each other. Photographs were exchanged and the British mothers began to feel quite superfluous. The American women prepared popcorn for them all. The Soviet women had brought an embroidered towel from the Ukraine and in traditional manner placed some fresh-baked bread and salt on the cloth inviting everyone to take a piece of bread and dip it in the salt as a sign of friendship. It was a very moving occasion. Lucy was presented with a tee-shirt stamped 'Mothers for Peace' and a little samovar.

The following morning the fifteen mothers divided into three teams of five and set off in three directions to tour the provinces: one group travelled around southern England, one group went to the north-west and North Wales, and the third journeyed to Yorkshire and Edinburgh. All three groups returned to London for the final two days. During their stay all the mothers stayed with families and in this way were able to come nearer to an understanding and appreciation of the British way of life.

The group that toured the south of England addressed their first large public meeting, fittingly with Lucy Behenna, Marion Mansergh and the Mayor of Crawley, at the Civic Centre in Crawley. The meeting completed a Peace Week there and two hundred people attended. Marion tried to sit in the first row of the audience but Lucy insisted that she came and sat on the platform with herself and the mothers. This group then went on to Southampton and the Isle of Wight where they were greeted at Cowes by children on a pontoon who sang 'I want to teach the world to sing in perfect harmony' and 'Peace flows like a river', then on to Exeter, Barnstaple and Bristol. The Soviet women spoke of the terrible suffering of the last war. They did not appeal to governments or blame them but asked ordinary people everywhere to make a determined effort at peace-making. The Americans spoke of the growing peace movement in their country and the support for the Nuclear Freeze plan. The group continued to Evesham, Overbury, Worthing and Brighton and it was noticeable that they attracted many people who were not involved in the peace movement. The British mothers provided hospitality so the Americans and Soviets spent much time together sharing journeys and home life and had time to learn more about each other.

Meanwhile the second group had gone north to Manchester where at once they were plunged into a meeting with a sophisticated audience asking quite penetrating questions. The American mothers seemed to have difficulty with some of the probing questions and the audience were disappointed by the Soviet acceptance of their government. This was part of the great learning process of the visits: to try to understand quite different political points of view. However the real value of the visits for many was in the informal contact rather than in the public meetings. They had been invited as mothers, rather than as political or disarmament experts and found a common concern for peace and a wide range of common attitudes. One memory of this tour was of the members of the three nations washing up together, managing, in the interests of international cooperation, to break several dishes in the process of finding common ground.

Despite religious, political and economic differences, not to mention the few odd thousand miles that separated them, they each shared the same fears for the safety of their families, their goals, a sense of humour and fearsome mothers-in-law. Fazu, one of the Russians, recited a poem she had written about motherhood; bejewelled and speaking in Russian, she moved her audience by the sincerity and depth of her feeling. They visited Preston and Wrexham, where they took part in a May Day rally as a peace group. They had several interviews with local radio and a big public meeting which was also linked with a German Mothers for Peace visit. On a visit to a primary school the following day the theme was paper cranes, as the children remembered the story of Sadako, the little Japanese girl in hospital with radiation sickness, who had been told that her wish would be granted if she could make 1,000 paper cranes. She began by wishing that she would get well again, but as she realized that this could not be, she decided to make her paper cranes for peace and wrote 'Peace' across the wings of each bird as she made it, wishing that it would take its message to all the four corners of the globe. She died before the 1,000 were completed, but her family and school friends made the remaining ones and now such paper cranes are a world-wide symbol of peace. The American and Soviet mothers made them with the English children, all sharing Sadako's hope for peace. After a brief visit to Chester, the guests were seen off on a train to London. A British mother reflected as they departed after this exhausting but valuable three days how necessary it was not to lose the momentum and resolved to build on these contacts and exchange information, breaking down the barriers to involve more mothers from more countries and enabling them to speak frankly with each other.

The Scottish party had started in Edinburgh and moved on to Leith and Peebles. The highlight of this visit was an evening of food, wine and music where everyone came to relax and enjoy themselves. When the music moved into the right mood Ljuba suddenly spun into the middle of the room and dazzled everyone with some fantastic dancing, even inspiring a Tweeddale partner into dances he did not know he knew; a magic moment that demolished all barriers. The group returned to more public meetings in Edinburgh, but behind the outward happenings was the quiet caring way everyone worked together making the most of all their abilities and opportunities and managing to establish contact with so many people. This group then went on to Leeds, Bradford and York, with more meetings in which the Russian women again talked mainly about the suffering and devastation they had experienced during the war and the Americans, including Billie-Rose Wright who had initiated 'Women to End War in the World', spoke more individually of their work for peace. In Leeds they sang together a Russian children's song:

Let there always be sunshine
Let there always be blue sky,
Let there always be Mummy,
Let there always be me.

On returning to London some of the mothers visited Greenham Common to honour the heroism of these women whose name was known in places as far apart as Dagestan and Arizona. There was a Civic Reception at County Hall in London in the evening and later a letter was written to the Secretary General of the United Nations from the mothers of all three nations expressing their strong desire for disarmament, for the future safety of their children and for the immediate relief of poverty in the developing countries.

Emotions ran high at the final gathering of the mothers at Hampstead Meeting House on Thursday 6th May. Lucy presented the visitors with two glass goblets reputed to have been used by Dickens in an English pub. One would find a home in the Soviet Women's Committee display in Moscow; the other would travel to Washington.

With their great sense of occasion, the Soviet delegation brought bread and salt on a tablecloth as a symbol of eternal friendship and mothers and friends of three nations broke and ate bread together. An American mother later commented how impressed she was by this ceremony offered by so-called 'atheist' women, because of the importance of salt and bread in her life as a Christian.

The northern party then led the singing with 'Let there always be sunshine' and 'It's a long way to Tipperary', (which the Soviet party knew well) whilst Ljuba and Fazu performed some Russian dances. Billie-Rose then led them into 'We shall overcome' and all present were drawn into a circle, arms round each other as they sang. For many this was the moving culmination of the visit. After an exchange of presents, all that remained was the sad parting and the fond farewells at the airport. They had all made deep friendships and felt a oneness and love for each other overriding national boundaries and political systems. Lucy's vision that mothers share a common bond was more than proved during the visits and many felt that each delegation took home with them in their hearts all the finest qualities of their so-called 'enemies'.

The British account of the experience emphasized that 'getting to know and understand people is an important step in learning to love them' and quoted Martin Luther King's words: 'We should love our enemies because love is the only force capable of transforming an enemy into a friend. We never get rid of an enemy by meeting hate with hate; we get rid of an enemy by getting rid of enmity. By its very nature, hate destroys and tears down; by its very nature love creates and builds up. Love transforms with redemptive power.'[10]

The account continued 'If the governments of the world will not take the lead in bringing about world peace then we, the ordinary people of all nations must do it. We must show that those who abuse human rights are more likely to respond to peaceful persuasion than to violent threat and that if we blow up ourselves and our children, then we shall have destroyed the world out of ignorance, arrogance and fear'. The account ended with the hope that before long all the mothers of the world would be mothers for peace, working to show that the arms race impoverishes the lives of all children and ultimately threatens their very existence.

Lucy and Marion must have felt very happy at this most successful outcome of their idea.

In September 1982 it was decided to further the work of Mothers for Peace by appointing a part-time worker, Pat Dale, to coordinate activities. The entire organization for the 1982 return visits had been handled by the mothers and helpers on a voluntary basis. It was hoped that many local groups would be formed, eager to make their own international contacts and fund one of their members to visit another country.

# 17
# *Tears and Rainbows*

In April 1983 Mothers for Peace hosted a week-long meeting in Birmingham for mothers from Sweden and Germany as well as the USA and USSR. Lucy's intention was that they should discuss how they might 'plan and work to change the ideas of their respective governments and peoples from fear and mistrust which promotes planning for war, to mutual understanding which will encourage planning for peace' and at the end of the week she described it as 'an inspiring occasion when we pulled up the weeds of ignorance and mistrust and planted seeds of hope and cooperation'.

One Swedish representative belonged to a Scandinavian organization called 'Kvinnor for Fred'—Women for Peace—which began with a torchlight procession in December 1979 protesting against nuclear power. Karin told of the first Peace March from Scandinavia through West Germany to Paris in the summer of 1981 and the following year to the Soviet Union. The participants were accused of being naive and told they would be used for Russian propaganda; they were asked what they could do for Afghanistan and Poland and what they knew about Soviet politics. 'However, 300 women from Scandinavia had something else in mind. They wanted to know how the Russians think and feel about the arms race, if they are frightened of nuclear weapons as the Western women are. They met friendliness everywhere, in Leningrad, Moscow, Minsk. They met with tears and embraces and love and returned to their own countries with addresses of their new friends.'[11]

The other Swedish representative, Inger, belonged to the movement 'The Future in our Hands' which was founded

Birmingham discussion week, April 1983

in Norway in 1974. 'Its first consideration was to foster understanding for a reduced personal consumption, for the benefit of an active policy of solidarity towards the world's poor majority'. This movement had more than 21,000 members and Inger felt very strongly the waste of resources on armaments while children die of hunger:

> If no change takes place, more than half of all the children now living are doomed to die of hunger and deficiency diseases before they reach adulthood—because a majority of the world's population does not even have enough food.
>
> In a world where the majority are suffering great need there are more important things we can produce than nuclear weapons, luxury, fashion and prestige goods. Reason must tell us that we can no longer emphasize materialistic values—if we are to solve the problems of today and tomorrow.[12]

Prudence from the USA spoke of the many different

women's peace movements in her country especially mentioning Betty Bumpers's 'Peace Links' and the Seneca Falls Women's Peace Encampment. She was also encouraged by the national 'Jobs with Peace Campaign'. With the realization that military spending is capital intensive but not job intensive, several trade unions were backing this as they aimed to ensure security of employment without relying on jobs related to nuclear weapons-making. They had also launched a massive and effective peace curriculum in the schools and were getting down to some serious consideration of conversion to a peacetime economy.

Viola and Vera from the Soviet Union reminded the meeting of the suffering of the last war when its fire consumed fifty-five million lives, among them twenty million from the USSR. They described the way women were working for peace in their country mainly through the Soviet Peace Fund which consisted of voluntary contributions from Soviet people. Women gave their earnings from what are known as 'work shifts for peace'. They spoke of the Peace Marches in which they had joined through Russian territory, from Stockholm to Minsk and from Moscow to Vienna.

The West Germans spoke of their Easter protest marches and Hertha referred to the World Organization of Mothers of All Nations, WOMAN, which was founded in 1946 by an American journalist, Dorothy Thompson, and based on her experiences in Germany after the First World War. Hertha said there were now several groups in Germany although the organization was banned in America under the McCarthy regime in the fifties. Now in Germany WOMAN was pressing for changes in text books to eliminate all references which would sow hatred and discord.

In the discussion afterwards there were disagreements but the atmosphere remained friendly, and paramount was the shared concern for disarmament. Perhaps the questions to Soviet mothers were less probing than they might have been but this reflected the sense of fair play as they were the only Eastern bloc representatives (a situation Mothers for Peace had especially tried to avoid). 'It was also because in some uncanny way the group dynamics naturally sought to bring out what we had in common rather than where we opposed each other.'

During the week there were various opportunities to meet women from the peace camps and a visit to Greenham was arranged. When American cruise missiles arrived at Greenham Common Air Base at the end of August 1981 a march began from South Wales to protest. After the march, several women set up camp outside the gates of the Air Base. By the spring of 1982 a decision had been taken to restrict the camp to women only and Greenham Common Women's Peace Camp—commonly referred to as 'the Greenham women', was firmly established, together with a supporting network, Women for Life on Earth. It was a camp which grew and attracted many women from many different backgrounds and with a variety of different beliefs, but all with the gut reaction that something had to be done to save the future. As Sarah Green wrote in a letter the following year:

> I think that most women are really in touch with what life is about. You can't even contemplate having a child without considering the value of that life and the struggle people have bringing up children, putting in all those hours and hours of caring. . . . You just can't contemplate all that being destroyed by some people's fear and difference in ideologies of different countries. It just doesn't make sense. Life is so much more precious than that. Also women can identify with women of Russia and Eastern bloc countries. We're just the same. A woman in Russia is the same as myself—the same emo-

tions, leading the same sort of life. In no way will I be part of anything that will murder her. The myth that's been around so long that we need armies, we need missiles, men must protect women and children from other men in other countries, that's just completely out of hand. Women must come and say 'We don't need this type of protection. It's this type of protection which is actually endangering our lives'. We have to find our own strength, ways of using energy whereby we can actually change the situation because it's a very small minority of people making these decisions, not taking account of people's lives—playing with our lives. The majority of people in this country don't want this. What we are doing here is a consciousness-raising thing, particularly for women, because most women don't take an active part in politics. They allow their lives to be run by rules and regulations, by parliament—mainly by the male structure. We can all come out and say 'You can't do this to us'.[13]

Jean from Molesworth Peace Camp and Angela from the Peace Chariot, Sheffield, explained to the meeting how Greenham and Molesworth had grown and developed and how the essential message was 'You have to do it for yourself—no one can do it for you'. Jean stressed that there is a need to think deeply about peace and to train for non-violent action but that basically 'as long as you are peaceful, you can do whatever feels right' Angela talked about the Peace Chariot and the need to provide a long-term peace community as people question their life styles on coming into contact with the peace movement.

The Birmingham meeting participants planned to hold a silent vigil at the main gate of Greenham and had asked friends and supporters to join them. They were excited at the thought of women from East and West joining together outside the base. Sadly Vera and Viola felt they could not come as there had been so many accusations that the camp was supported by 'the Communists' and they in no way wanted to occasion further smears. The others understood what they meant and realized that it had been a serious and probably a wise decision for them but all were very saddened by it. The Greenham women stressed that they were strong enough to withstand such lies, but the decision had been taken. The women arrived at Greenham in the pouring rain. This made it difficult to introduce people and talk but as they stood in their dripping clothes just for an hour they were able to identify closely with the women living up against the fence all the time. The actress Susannah York and her niece joined them. As the vigil was due to begin women stood on either side of the entrance and Lucy was helped from the coach by her Greenham sisters, walking with them under a huge umbrella up to the gate. 'Silence fell and deepened although lorries and cars still rolled into the camp and police chatted and laughed at the gate. Prue delivered a letter they had written to the Base Commander explaining how they felt. Children played and splashed in puddles.' It was their future that the mothers were thinking about.

Many have a poignant memory of Lucy, a tiny little figure hobbling up to one of the policemen at the gate and holding out her hand in a gesture of friendship. He, young and probably unsure of himself, turned away in rejection—or perhaps with a muddled sense of duty. They all stood there in that relentless rain, tears flowing, knowing deep down that if governments plan such weapons of destruction, then the police would have to protect the weapons and not the people. They remembered the words of Joanna Macey: 'We are all part of a vast web. As we allow ourselves to feel our pain for the world we reach our inter-connectedness with each other.'[14]

Vera and Viola had not been physically present at the

camp but they had sent letters of support and badges to put on the fence. When the women all joined up in Oxford Viola told how they had been with them at the vigil by leaving the museum and standing out in the rain to join the others in spirit.

Still feeling like drowned rats they all attended a reception at the Oxford Town Hall where Lucy was able to meet an old friend from CND days, Olive Gibbs.

As they drove through the rain back to Birmingham a rainbow shone out in front of them and Prue began to sing Pete Seeger's song:

> O had I a golden thread and needle so fine
> I'd weave a magic strand of rainbow design, of rainbow design . . .
> Show my brothers and my sisters my rainbow design
> Bind up this sorry world with hand and mind, hand, heart and mind . . .[15]

For some this song became the symbol of the week: tears and rainbows. One of the deepest impressions of the week was the quality of the relationships built up and the discovery of how much they all had in common. They were aware of the real political differences between East and West and felt that perhaps they should have discussed these more than they did. But to discuss the more painful differences more time was needed. By the end of the week the relationships were strong enough for people not to feel threatened by discussion of these issues. Maybe government negotiators could learn from such an approach, but the group members were not there as government negotiators, they had come together as mothers and women to break down the barriers between them and to share their common concern for a safe future for their children. By these criteria the week was an overwhelming success and looking round at the many happy faces they wondered why their message seemed so alien to so many other people. The final evening ended standing in a circle holding hands and singing the Greenham chant:

You can't kill the spirit
She is like a mountain
Old and strong
She goes on and on and on . . .

The chant was repeated so its power slowly grew until the air was heavy with the peaceful strength of women.

# 18
# *Coping With Old Age*

As Mothers for Peace expanded the work-load had grown enormously. The work not only involved planning the visits and arranging itineraries and hospitality for mothers coming to Britain, but there were also speaking tours to be worked out so that as many people as possible should be able to share the experiences of the mothers. Pat Dale, employed part-time to coordinate the work, made over a room in her house as an office. From here she also produced the quarterly newsletter, answered correspondence, keeping in touch with peace groups all over the world and coped with media enquiries. In 1983 the Joseph Rowntree Charitable Trust made a grant to pay a small salary for three years but money was still needed to pay expenses and Lucy suggested a number of fund-raising ideas. Until 1984 (when the Committee asked her to become President of Mothers for Peace) she remained the treasurer. After the first expedition the mothers were involved in raising their own fares.

The founding of Mothers for Peace at first aroused much interest among the other residents at Ifield. But when the publicity increased some of them came to find it a little tiresome, especially since the telephone was in constant use with calls for Lucy or Marion. However they all, as Quakers, had a basic interest in peacemaking and some of them were very supportive.

Lucy still travelled up to London for meetings and took a full part in CND, Mothers for Peace, yoga classes and other activities in Crawley. She wrote in a letter to a friend:

> Folk ask me if there is anything to do here? This is Friday's programme:
>
> 11.00 am Discussion group. 'Peace slowly'.

3.30 pm Visit the residents' shop for fruit mainly
4.00 pm Different discussion group (visiting speaker)
Sunday 9.00 am–4.00 pm a special day's conference at Friends House.
Tuesday evening: visit local theatre.
Sandwich in work and correspondence and look after Mothers for Peace.
Can't say life's dull!

She would go off to London for the day or on one occasion to visit Stonehenge simply leaving a note to say that she would probably be back the following day and finding herself a bed and breakfast.

Lucy enjoyed the good things in life. She used pretty cups and saucers and loved her food. She was very sad when she had to give up cakes and biscuits because of a mild form of diabetes. (This may have been brought on by the shock of Dorothy's stroke.) In fact she was very remiss about her diet and often did not tell her hostesses about her diabetes, especially when there were cakes or puddings on the menu. She was also very particular about her clothes although her dress was sometimes surprising. Marion Thorpe recalls how when she came to spend a weekend at Worthing she appeared completely in white: hat, dress and shoes, 'like a little Edwardian lady, gaily determined to enjoy the seaside'. She bought her first pair of trousers at the age of eighty-eight. Lucy used to enjoy a slight tipple and loved going to the Mayor's receptions. Cathy Ashton remembers how she got mildly drunk on white wine at the party they gave when she left CND's head office. On the other hand she had no time for possessions as such. The many gifts which were given to her by visitors or mothers returning from abroad usually found their way on to the Oxfam stall. She always used to be knitting, usually black or grey socks or blanket squares for Oxfam.

Caroline Herring, the wife of the Warden at Ifield, often

used to drive Lucy to the station, to meetings or to Gatwick and knew her well. She remembers on one occasion when Lucy was going up to a Mothers for Peace meeting in London she was very wheezy and confided to Caroline on the train that she had fallen just before leaving and thought that she had broken a couple of ribs but wouldn't say anything about it in case she was stopped from going. She told Caroline about an occasion when she was young and had fallen down between the train and the platform; she just managed to hang on to the door which was swinging open and the train couldn't start until she was rescued. Lucy was always very trusting. She knew that someone would always come to her help if she needed them—and they did. On one occasion she came up to London for a meeting and was standing at the bus stop for a bus home when two policemen stopped in their car; the last bus had gone and they were concerned about this tiny, frail old lady so they took her all the way home. Lucy seemed to lead a charmed life. Coming to Birmingham for an AGM on a Saturday morning she had arranged with a friend to meet her at Victoria and accompany her. She simply forgot this and arrived at Bull Street Friends Meeting House on Friday evening wanting a bed. Fortunately a host was quickly found. She was so small she could stand up in a London taxi and Alison Tyas remembers lifting her down out of a taxi on to the pavement.

In 1983 Marion became quite ill and had to spend some weeks in a nursing home. Lucy was having difficulty with her sight and confessed to Pat Dale in a letter that she was 'babying' herself these days by coming up to Euston on a Friday night for a Saturday meeting in Southport and using a hotel for bed and breakfast in London. She was also thrilled to hear about Pat's proposed visit to Siberia and wrote:

. . . having tried for years at Evening School (while teaching) to learn Russian, you have my deepest sympathy in its being a difficult language to master. It had one consolation: once the sounds of the letters have been grasped it's fairly consistent in the pronunciation, not like our own erratic one.

And it will pay off a hundredfold. I could just manage to ask 'How many children?' and it pleased the Russian woman enormously.

If you can manage to get a set of Linguaphone records, they are reliable and helpful. Sorry I gave another learner my set.

Have you heard how Mao taught his peasant army to read? As they went in single file over the mountain road, each man carried on his back first a letter and later a word. By staring at the man ahead he learnt.

A canny student I knew adopted the idea by stringing a line across his room.

A new word he wrote on a piece of cardboard, English one side and Russian the other. He hung his placards on the line—first learning and then checking his memory.

Increasingly Lucy was finding it difficult to come to terms with her failing eyesight and her lack of memory and accuracy in handling the Mothers for Peace accounts, which worried her greatly. She wrote a letter on Good Friday 1984 saying '. . . the day my sister died, so to help me forget sad thoughts I've decided to sit down and write to you.' Later in the letter she confesses: 'What a tiresome business growing old is, not only to oneself but one's friends and relations and other folk. Most unquakerly, I know, but if Providence wanted me to carry on Mothers for Peace, why on earth didn't he leave me my sight unimpaired?'

The cataracts in her eyes impaired her sight considerably by this time and she also needed to wear a hearing aid. Apart from diabetes Lucy also suffered from arthritis. The latter was probably eased by yoga lessons for the elderly which were available for all residents, the teacher being Margaret Graham, the daughter of the founder of Ifield. Yet despite these physical handicaps, Lucy was the first to give encouragement to others with the reminder that 'a journey of a thousand miles begins with a single step'. She would urge that 'the work must go on. It was founded in faith and will continue in faith'.

# 19
# *Visits to the USSR, 1984*

During 1984 Mothers for Peace made two visits to the Soviet Union, and a third delegation, including Lucy, visited the USA.

In April Sally Brown, Elizabeth Cave and Jill Stow visited Moscow, Minsk and Kalinin (on the Volga to the north-west of Moscow), being accompanied throughout as guide, interpreter and friend by Vera Soboleva, a senior staff member at the Soviet Women's Committee, who had participated in the Birmingham meeting the previous year.

During the two days which they spent in Minsk they were very conscious of the difference between knowing the facts and figures about war and being close to the reality of suffering experienced by the people of Byelorussia, of which Minsk is the capital. Here they met two women war veterans: one had worked as a nurse at the Front when she was only thirteen, the other had lost both her children at the beginning of the war and had then got a job as a maid in the house of a Nazi general and blown it up. Both told of appalling horrors they had witnessed. The British women asked them, 'After going through all this, do you worry about the massive build-up of terrible new weapons in your country?' Their reply was vehement. 'We must never again be undefended. We must never again suffer as we suffered then.'

That afternoon the mothers were taken to see the war memorial at Khatyn. Khatyn was a village in which all the inhabitants who had not left to fight were herded into a barn by the Nazis and burned alive. Some got out and tried to run away. All were gunned down except for one man, Kaminsky. At the entrance to the site of the village there was a massive statue of him holding his dead son. Nine thousand villages in Byelorussia were burned down and a quarter of the population killed. One of the mothers wrote later: 'There is an eternal flame beside a silver birch in the centre of the site and every thirty seconds, day and night, a bell tolls, flat, cold and mournful. The memorial is in the country, surrounded by fields and woods; the contrast between the sunshine and beauty of its natural surroundings and this place of grief, evil and death epitomized the contrast between the world of love, warmth and life which we want to hand on to our children and the evil, darkness and death of which the arms race is a symptom.'

Later they visited a school where a class of nine-year-old children, just beginning to learn English, asked them questions. Jill gave them a book made by her daughter's class and they all said in slow careful English: 'We send love and happiness to Emma and her friends.' She found it hard to face the fact that western missiles were trained on those bright-faced little children.

Their two days in Kalinin gave the mothers the opportunity to see homes, workplaces and leisure facilities as well as a state farm outside the town boundary. Kalinin is not habitually visited by tourists and they went there because Ljuba Parfenova, who had visited Britain in 1982 at the invitation of Mothers for Peace, wanted to return the hospitality personally—which she did in full measure.

Ljuba was a textile worker and the Soviet Women's Committee representative for Kalinin. Among the places she had chosen for the mothers to visit was a nursery attached to a complex of textile factories. When the children came indoors Elizabeth gave a class of five-year-olds a book made by her five-year-old daughter's class. The teacher held it up as the children crowded round, while she read the Russian translation of the text and showed the photographs. She said to the British women over the children's heads: 'How could these children want to kill each other?'

Presentation of the book from Elizabeth Cave's daughter's class to children in the nursery at Kalinin.

The mothers left the school a copy of the Quaker poster with photos of British and Soviet children and the words: 'We can learn to live in peace if you give us a future.'

The mothers spent a convivial evening with Ljuba's

family and friends recognizing that there was no need for people in the Soviet Union to think 'just like us', before we can recognize their common humanity and live in the spirit of it.

Several times during their ten-day visit the mothers raised the matter of human rights, pointing out it was one of the issues which made westerners fear the nature of Soviet society; each time the response was to question why issues of peace and disarmament were so constantly linked to the internal affairs of the Soviet Union. It was explained that dissidents got into trouble because they broke the law. For their part, the Russians deplored some of the things that go on in Britain, such as unemployment, which they consider as a violation of the basic human right to work. It was also pointed out that the Soviet democratic state had only existed for sixty years, whereas the British had had their parliament for three hundred years. They didn't claim to see their country as perfect, but it was developing. They said they knew they had made mistakes and were prepared to differ on the ways each country saw its respective society.

The official the mothers met at the Soviet Peace Committee in Moscow stressed that the arms race was far too great a strain on the Soviet economy and pointed out that they had no private arms dealers making profits out of arms sales. The mothers recognized that the Soviet Peace Committee had many limitations—that it was prestigious and influential, and perhaps, by the same token, too conservative and not critical enough of government policy—but they also recognized and admired some sort of commitment to educate people for peace and to 'promote peaceful public attitudes'.

In response to their request to see something of the life of the church, the mothers were taken to Zagorsk, where the Russian Orthodox Church maintains a monastery, a seminary and an academy for the education and training of monks and parish priests and which is a centre for Christian worship. They learnt that the state contributed to the upkeep of the magnificent historic buildings as works of art and the church used them. They were there on Easter Eve and saw many believers preparing the churches for evening services and queueing for the blessing of their Easter food. (Although the Communist Party is opposed to religion, the state in principle is not.) They were pleasantly surprised to discover, when they asked what the thousands of worshippers would do at the end of the Easter services at three or four o'clock in the morning, that special trains would be running to take them home.

Sally, Jill and Elizabeth realized that they had seen only a very small part of life in the Soviet Union and that what they had seen was chosen for being positive, but they did not think that the wool had been pulled over their eyes and felt sure their visit was worthwhile. They had given and received loving attention and had acted on their conviction that 'if we do not share our planet we are tacitly supporting developments that may well end in its destruction. As mothers, as human beings, we have to live in the spirit that takes away the occasion for wars'.

In October the same year a much larger delegation of ten mothers (two of them grandmothers) went to Moscow, Kirghizia and Tadzhikistan for nine days, again as guests of the Soviet Women's Committee. They came from all parts of the British Isles and represented a wide range of peace groups. Between them they were also linked to Amnesty International, UNA and the Peace Tax Campaign as well as political parties, churches and women's groups and organizations. In addition they represented a wide spectrum of personality, background and experience. Their individual approaches to peace-making and disarmament ranged from conventional work through political channels right across the board to nonviolent direct action. But they were united in their desire to build on the foundations of trust and friendship already established by the visits of previous Mothers for Peace, and surprised by the cohesion achieved as a group, although they met only twice before the trip. They were met at the airport by four guides and interpreters, Vera, Masha, Ludmilla and Leona, who proved to be not only attentive and thoughtful hostesses but a mine of information. The following day the group split up: half travelled to Firunze in Khirgizia, which borders on China, and the other half to Dushambe, the capital of Tadzhikistan, the most southern republic of the Soviet Union, separated only by mountains from Afghanistan. The flights to each of these places took longer than the flight from Heathrow to Moscow. They were in Central Asia.

In Dushambe the mothers visited both a Russian-speaking school specializing in English and a Khirghiz-speaking school. Both had 'Club of International Friendship' groups which produced peace work. Then they visited the Cardiology Institute where the professor told them in detail about his work and made the point that doctors in the Soviet Union undertake as part of their Hippocratic oath to work against nuclear war. He reminded them that doctors throughout the world were uniting against nuclear weapons.

On the Friday afternoon they visited a peace meeting outside the University. They felt rather uneasy and vulnerable at the front of a large meeting at which the speeches were supporting the 'peaceful aims of the government' and a veteran soldier stood in uniform to speak about the tragedy of the last war. However, when Margaret spoke in Russian about her fears for her family in England and when the mothers sang 'We are women, we are strong' there was a visible change in the women at the meeting. Then a group of students sang: 'We shall overcome' and they were united in their desire for peace, but 'with a realization of how easy it is for our different ways of thinking to set up barriers between us'.

On the last evening, they sat down together, Khirgizian, Russian and British mothers and talked of their strengths and aims, sharing them with one another. There was a real feeling of trust and understanding. The visit provided one of the mothers with one of her most treasured quotes – from the deputy leader of the municipal Soviet, who said: 'The preservation of peace depends upon how women bring up their children and husbands.'

The group who went to Tadzhikistan wrote a very full account of all aspects of Soviet life there, which can be found in the pamphlet *Mothers for Peace* published in 1985.[16] Perhaps the most interesting aspect of their visit was to learn of the changes in the role of women in this area over the last sixty years.

Peace and disarmament issues were also on their agenda. The British women heard that Soviet children are asking their mothers: 'Are we going to have nuclear war?' This they could entirely relate to. Meeting and talking to the people who were officially their enemies, seeing their children laughing, dancing and generally enjoying themselves, the idea of even threatening to drop a nuclear missile on any of them became even more unthinkable and crazy. Time and again they heard of the terrible sufferings of the last war and the determination that it should never happen again and realized why the Soviet desire for peace ran side by side with a high level of defence.

A meeting with the Tadzhik Friendship Society nearly broke up in disarray as they tried to explain that people in the West felt just as threatened as did those in the East, and that some people in the West had expressed scepticism about the sincerity of both American and Soviet governments' assertions that they wanted disarmament. This was too much for the President and further discussion was useless.

One thing that was emphasized as a barrier between West and East, when a meeting was later held in Moscow with the Soviet Peace Committee, was the apparent lack of freedom of the ordinary Soviet citizen to travel to non-Communist countries. Reasons were given for this, such as difficulty of changing roubles on the international monetary market. However, the mothers were able to penetrate a barrier of disinterest to press for a party of thirty Russian women to come to Britain the following year and stay in the homes of Mothers for Peace.

The mothers returned feeling that the main value of their visit had been in the ordinary people they had met—'people with husbands, wives, parents, children; people with a different outlook, culture and priorities from our own, but nevertheless with hopes, fears, joys and aspirations; most of all, people to whom we could relate on many levels'. They felt they had gained an insight into a Soviet way of life and a Soviet way of thinking. This helped their understanding of differences: the Soviet respect for their government, compared with the more flippant British attitude to politicians generally; differences in the concept of human rights—individual freedom matters less, but the opportunities for work, education and suitable accommodation are a state duty to provide and a citizen's right to receive. They found that emphasis on the 'glory of work' made work almost an end in itself, but at the same time there was a non-competitive, collective pride in the achievements of an individual worker or group of workers.

They came away feeling that they wanted to go back, that they wanted to tell others about their experiences and that 'if only a fraction of the time, effort and money spent on "defence" could be used instead on the promotion of men, women and children in both East and West getting to know each other as people, some of the overwhelming problems with which the world is faced might, quite suddenly, disappear.'

# 20
# *Visit to the USA, 1984*

The invitation for a group from Mothers for Peace to visit the USA came from Quakers at Sandy Springs and specifically asked for Lucy to be one of the delegation. She would be able to stay at the residential home for the elderly. Some had expected that Lucy would decline, being now eighty-eight years old, but she accepted with enthusiasm. She wrote to Pat Dale, 'I shall feel like "royalty" receiving visitors. I saw Doctor before accepting. Travelling with a group my eyes won't matter and the Americans are very diet-conscious. But mine is a simple one.' Marion, now recovered from her illness, was probably more agile than Lucy but she didn't want all the publicity which such a journey would involve. One of the residents at Ifield remembers Lucy suddenly appearing in her room one morning wearing black trousers which she had bought for her American trip and for her yoga classes. She said that she'd bought them to match her tweed coat and red twin set. She had never been to Heathrow before but told the others that she would meet them in the departure lounge and that her luggage would be one medium-sized suit case (red leatherette) and a large handbag (plus stick and goggles).

So in a late April heat-wave Lucy arrived at Dulles airport for a twelve-day visit together with Jan Toms, mother of two from the Isle of Wight, Patsy Cumming, grandmother of five and art teacher from Scotland, Cath Barker, mother of two sons and district nurse from Cumbria and Sylvia Baker, also with two sons, a teacher from Somerset.

On this trip they were to be joined by two mothers from Denmark and four from the Soviet Union. The Danish delegates, Lise and Marianne, were also at the airport where they were all met warmly by Deedie Runkle and Betty Bumpers along with other members of Washington 'Peace Links'. They drove out through lush countryside and the red, pink and white blossoms of dogwood and azaleas to Sandy Springs to meet their host families and the group of Quakers who had organized the trip.

The following day the four Soviet delegates arrived after a journey of thirty-five hours. They had had to come through Canada since the US was banning all Aeroflot flights from the Soviet Union. Head of the delegation was Galina Semyonova from Moscow, member of the Soviet Women's Committee and editor of *Peasant Woman* magazine. Also from Moscow was Marina Moskvina, a senior staff member of the Soviet Women's Committee; Natasha Alexandrova, a senior teacher of English who came from Leningrad and Gulnora Akhrorova, a secondary school principal from Dushambe in Tadzhikistan.

Before the British women left home people had asked them whether they thought the trip would do any good. They had all said 'Perhaps' but at the back of their minds were questions and doubt. Would contact established between a small number of people justify the cost? They also questioned their own qualifications, wondering whether they knew enough about the arms race, the Soviet Union and America, whether they were articulate enough and had the right to go and 'preach' to the American people. However they soon realized that their original affirmation was right because they found that the learning process was a two-way communication. They learned that the fundamental reason for the visit—bridge-building between people—was the most valuable part and one into which they could put all their energy.

The visiting delegates all spoke that evening at the Meeting House in Sandy Springs and it became apparent that their perceptions of war and motivations for being in the peace movement were very different. The British women spoke of the deployment of cruise missiles and the presence of the Women's Peace Camp at Greenham Common while the Soviet women spoke about their past experiences of war.

Describing her individual motivation for joining the peace movement, Patsy Cumming spoke movingly of how, having been widowed for the second time, she had lost the will to live and her daughter provoked her into action by asking what she intended to do about the threat to the world from nuclear weapons. When Patsy claimed that there was nothing she could do being 'only a grain of sand', her daughter retorted that grains of sand covered the earth. Patsy read aloud a harrowing excerpt from John Hersey's book *Hiroshima*[17] which for her had been a catalyst; audience and delegates alike could not hide their tears at the tragedy of the mother searching for her child in the ruins and then holding her for nine hours before she died.

Natasha said she was too young to remember the last war but she did remember visiting her Granny's grave and learning that she had died of starvation during the 900 days' siege of Leningrad. 'I love my two sons and want them to grow up safely,' she said and then pointing at a baby in the audience she said simply 'and I love your baby too.'

Lucy impressed them all with a simple account of her naturally rebellious nature. She said that the 1914–18 war had denied her the role of wife and mother because her might-have-been husband was killed, along with four million other young men. Since then she had worked to prevent such a horror happening again.

Cath and Sylvia spoke about the impact of cruise missiles and assured the Americans that the peace camp at Greenham was still a presence and an inspiration to the peace movement. Cath said that a recent Amnesty International conference had disclosed that during April 1984, 300 women from Greenham were in prison and since 1981 some 4,000 people had been arrested for taking part in some form of peaceful protest throughout Britain. The audience were astonished to learn of the 135 American bases in Britain and the 90,000 personnel.

The Russian women spoke of the last war—not one family in the Soviet Union had escaped without losing a loved one: twenty million dead; twenty million more homeless; 1,700 cities obliterated; how could they ever want another war? At this point Marina, interpreting for Galina, was so overcome by emotion that she could not continue and silently weeping she sat down. Jan put her arm round her and felt her stifled sobs. Marina, who had appeared so professional and so aloof, was weeping publicly for other people's grief.

In contrast to the emotional and almost religious quality of the public meeting held by the Quakers, the group also encountered other aspects of the American peace movement in Washington exemplified by the Wives of Senators and Congressmen who supported the Nuclear Freeze Proposals (a bilateral agreement to halt the testing, deployment and production of all nuclear weapons as a first step towards reduction). Their aim was to reach a new audience of women in the mainstream of American life who had not previously been active. In 1982 the women had been attacked verbally on the floor of the Senate by a Senator claiming they were Soviet-controlled, openly sympathetic with and advocating a Communist foreign policy, and that they were dupes and traitors. To the British women it had an all too familiar ring. At the same time they were struck by the lack of knowledge about the British political process and the peace movement in Britain. The notion that the Russians had a Peace Committee, funded by a Peace Fund from voluntary donations, was a totally new idea to the

Americans and alerted them to the contrast in historical experience of war: they recognized that actual knowledge of invasion, of concentration camps, led ordinary Soviet people to take the issue of peace very seriously indeed.

Overall the British mothers were heartened by their meetings in Washington. Since the first trip to the USA by Mothers for Peace in 1981 there appeared to have been an increase in public awareness of the nuclear issue and the Freeze Campaign had caught the imagination of the population.

After four days in Washington the party split into two groups: Cath, Jan, Marina and Galina set off by car to Pennsylvania whilst the others flew to the Rockies.

Cath and Jan found they could relate more easily to the Russian women, now that they were in a small group. They spent a morning in a high school with seventeen and eighteen-year-olds who felt that nuclear weapons would be used and there wasn't anything they could do about it. It was a sad morning but the mothers hoped they had given the students something to think about. One disturbing feature of the high school pupils and teachers encountered was that they expressed a rather uniform view that the United States had a right to intervene in the policies of other countries in order to defend American 'liberty'. The word 'liberty' was never defined but sparked off fierce patriotic emotion. In Old Lyme, Connecticut, after a lecture on the arms race at a high school, the four women split up and took a class of children to discuss the lecture. The Russian women were quite shocked at the information given to the children. They protested that the children were being educated towards war rather than towards peace. It seemed to open their eyes to the urgency of the arms build up and its inherent dangers. When they got back to Washington Galina and Marina initiated a letter, which all the delegates signed, appealing to all governments for an end to the arms race.

Meanwhile, in the snowbound Rockies, the other group was being hosted by Denver American Friends Service Committee, whose work was concentrated on their opposition to the Rocky Flats Nuclear Weapons Plant and its associated contamination. After two days they drove on to Boulder, to the home of the Rocky Mountains Peace Centre, a new venture aimed at educating activists in the theories of nonviolence and looking at the causes of war and the possibility of conversion of the armaments industry to peaceful uses. Boulder had a very sophisticated population; the Centre of Advanced Technology was there and it was the home of research on nuclear winter theories. The group whom the mothers met were engaged on setting up a Soviet sister project and trying to twin Boulder with a Russian city.

Marianne and Gulnora visited a high school. Here Gulnora, on learning that an Afghan boy was among the pupils, asked to speak with him. The boy, when he discovered Gulnora's nationality, refused to talk with her. However he spoke freely to Marianne in English and said his uncle, brothers and cousin had been killed by Russian troops. He had hidden in a tree for four days until it was safe to come down. Gulnora retorted that Afghanistan had asked Russian troops to come to her aid in order to subdue 'subversive' forces. The mothers felt that peace links were not achieved by this encounter. But they did learn a little of the official Soviet attitude to Afghanistan. After two days in the mountains visiting schools, clinics and talking to the general public, the group divided again.

Sylvia, Gulnora and Natasha set off next to the state of Idaho. In Boise they found a soft gentle green landscape of lakes and pastureland. The hosting group were the Boise Women for Peace, a group made up of young mothers. The women were very interested in alternative life styles and were educating their children at home or in progressive schools. They had come together in 1982. They were a very cohesive organization, because they had an activity which gave them a clear purpose—they made friendship quilts. In 1982 they made their first quilt for the people of Alitus in Lithuania. Since then they had made ten quilts and when the group arrived they were working on a quilt for the people of Leningrad. The quilt was composed of squares sewn from drawings by Soviet and American children. One of the founder members of the group said: 'Working with a needle and thread creates something new—it is like stitching the world together and making peace between peoples'.

A further important group in Idaho were the Canyon County Citizens for Peace who focused attention on the 'White Train' which carries enough fission material for ten Hiroshima bombs from the munitions plant in Amarillo, Texas, through Idaho en route to Bangor, Washington, and the nuclear base for Trident submarines. The Citizens had an alert system, symbolically stopped the train and held monthly vigils along the track.

Meanwhile Patsy, Marianne and Lise were encountering different groups with different emphases in the vast, flat windswept landscape of Iowa. Patsy discovered that the peace group there was the twin of her own peace group back in Tweeddale: born at the same time, it had developed along identical lines, encountering the same difficulties and finding the same strengths. They had several meetings here and attended a rally before flying on to Kansas where they were met by a deputation of children singing a moving song of peace. It was in Kansas that they were invited to a luxurious dinner at the Danish Consulate and reflected how wide and diverse the peace movement was in America and how it encompassed all kinds of people. Next day they had lunch with professional and business women and Joyce Olsen, the hostess, felt motivated to start a fund to raise money to bring women from Hiroshima or developing countries to America on future Mothers for Peace trips. This pleased the group as they had spoken very strongly for the needs of the developing countries and felt that in a sense they were all, since 1945, children of Hiroshima. In Kansas, too, the women met the Governor John Carlin and his wife Karen, who had been galvanized into action by seeing the making of the film *The Day After*, which had been filmed in her home district. The final meeting was the getting together of church groups and 'Scientists and Physicians for Social Responsibility'. The mothers felt rather inadequate for this challenge, but it turned out to be a satisfying meeting as the doctors and scientists were amazed at the amount of radioactive discharge into the Irish Sea from Sellafield and the European women were able to tell them much about the situation regarding contamination.

After seven days' intense travelling the three groups, eleven women in all, reassembled late on Saturday night at William Penn House in Washington. Here they spent some time hearing news from each group and sharing ideas of the way forward. Out of this discussion they decided to make a Joint Statement of Intent condemning the nuclear arms race, to be sent to their respective governments and the United Nations.

In Washington their final thoughts turned to the way the trip had developed; one important factor was the way each group had discovered its own cohesion and voice, sharing confidences and hazarding guesses as to what was going to happen next. They recalled how shocked the Russian women had been by a hospital in Pennsylvania which charged up to 4,750 dollars a day, and a junior school with fees of 3,000 dollars a year. The West European women saw how the women from the Soviet Union valued an ideology which regarded health and education as a social responsibility of the government and available to all regardless of the ability to pay. The Americans on the other hand had a history of individual pioneering and stressed achieving individually as a way of attaining jobs, health, housing and education. The contrast in histories was also apparent in the way the Russian women spoke so often about World War II; they justified their own arms build-up by a fear of invasion and did not recognize they were also guilty of war-mongering.

The British mothers were also interested in the way the Americans perceived the Soviet women and were surprised by American ignorance. Such questions as 'How did you manage to get out?' and 'Did you buy your clothes when you got here?' were asked, both questions amazing to the recipients. The American audiences were very anxious to learn and their eager questioning came because they were so clearly starved of any opportunity to make personal contact with people from the Soviet Union. Another impression, gained in response to American probing, was that the Soviet women were very defensive—no doubt in part because of the misconceptions about their way of life. While the British were freely criticizing their government, the Soviet women were unwilling to admit to any weakness or mistakes by their administration. Their reluctance to criticize could be seen as fear of dissent, but was also perhaps more a reluctance due both to loyalty to their country and its past struggles and to belief in loyalty to the community's achievements.

The mothers felt the need to share their perceptions of American society with their hosts and some of the most valuable moments came after the various evening functions when they chatted about what they thought and felt. Those shared evenings taught them a lot about America and certainly made them ashamed of any anti-American sentiment which had crept into their feelings before they left home.

In many instances the Mothers for Peace delegates did sense that they were building bridges between two great nations and, as Europeans, felt more objective about both social systems and able to appreciate the strengths and weaknesses of their policies. They concluded:

> Both sides—Russian and American—are loyal to their country's values and histories—and rightly so, but the cold war has frozen national responses and feelings and denied the possibility of curiosity and comprehension: values and attitudes that might not sit too comfortably together are exaggerated to simple caricature and implacable opposition. The result is that so much natural humanity is lost and understanding and trust diminished.
>
> However, there appeared to be many signs for hope in the future; the children's drawings—from Russia and America—are a powerful symbol of how small-scale attempts at friendship, such as the quilt, can generate so much good feeling and understanding. The desire to twin Russian and American cities offers an exchange of perspectives which is also a sign of hope, and the practical steps of arranging such goodwill visits generates an interest and heart-searching by local American communities, which is all helping to break barriers of fear and suspicion. Hopefully, it begins to thaw the frozen responses and open up minds and hearts to a desire for peace.

America has had its own tragedies and on our last day in Washington we visited the Vietnam memorial. This brought home to us all the futility of war. The many dazed visitors wept privately, some for personal loss, others for the waste of human life on such a vast scale.

How to make sure that such wars are not repeated? Looking at our small group and thinking of all the people we had talked to, we knew that in the vast majority the will is there. We simply need the courage to make peaceful co-existence and not confrontation our way of life.[18]

# 21
# *Peace Garden*

Lucy was eager to tell everyone about her time in the States. She struggled over to Bethnal Green for a meeting soon after getting home, but privately admitted it was very tiring and she could not attempt anything like that again. Sylvia Baker was asked to address the Mothers for Peace group in Godalming.

Lucy's tiredness was hardly surprising as by this time she was eighty-eight. She had just celebrated her 21st birthday! Jim Norman, one of the members of Godalming Meeting, realized that since Lucy was born in a leap year on February 29th and there was no leap year in 1900, this would be only her 21st birthday. He arranged for a 21st birthday greeting to be given to her by the Meeting. Mothers for Peace gave her a birthday party at their committee meeting and Wendy Franklin baked a cake with 21 candles. Despite her diabetes Lucy enjoyed a large chunk.

Until about this time Lucy had been very 'motherly' towards her 'mothers'. She was very forceful at times but always full of praise and very appreciative. Rarely was she cross with any one. Her enthusiasm carried them along and she was always allowed to be 'in charge' (although they usually got their way). But now she was beginning to lose her grasp and was like a little innocent child whom they had to protect and help in and out, up and down, and for whom they had to make all the arrangements. She would doze through meetings but was always determined to come and not to miss anything.

In the summer she went to stay with her friend Joan Castwood. On Sunday morning after breakfast she saw the roses from the window and went out to the terrace to look at them more closely, but missed her footing on the step and broke her leg. Roy Farrant, arriving to take them to Meeting, found her sitting there in great distress not because of her pain but because she felt herself to be such a nuisance in preventing Joan from going to Meeting. (She was as stoical as her sister Dorothy, who broke her toe just before a group photograph was taken but did not mention it until the session was finished.) Lucy's accident meant two months in hospital and a replacement hip. Although she was in a hospital near Ifield and many friends came to visit her, Lucy found the time very irksome and in August wrote to Joan:

> I had a 'gloomy' fit; the 20th seems so slow in coming and I'm O so tired of being a 'patient' with no 'freedom'. One is just a 'parcel' shunted hither and thither at the nurses' will. One stays 'put' so much of the time. But I am mobile again and can stroll in the grounds and even call a taxi to do some shopping. Our warden has come with me to my flat in Penn Court and discussed various ways to make life there easier. ... Everybody is most helpful and I really do think that folks understand that, however good a nursing home is, one prefers one's own home, plus the work.
>
> ... I'm learning to 'walk' again. Find my balance is not good, but with exercise I'm sure it will return. In myself I feel very well and long to be up and doing again'

A week later she was back in her flat again but was writing to Joan, 'I think it was one of the Catholic saints or St Francis who spoke of "the little miseries of life". Well I'm suffering from one at present.' She had lost Joan's letter. Earlier in the year she had felt unable to continue as treasurer of Mothers for Peace. She was no longer able to keep a grasp on the figures and this naturally worried her. Jan Toms took on the post.

Soon after this Elma Harland was going to a peace meeting in London and, as she went down the platform at

Euston, she saw Lucy sitting in an open-doored carriage. She was waiting for a wheel chair. Elma went with her in a taxi to Victoria but when they got there no wheel chair was available so Lucy said she would lean on a large luggage trolley which she pushed along very slowly. When they got to the platform the ticket collector said 'Hurry up, the train is just going'. Elma pointed out that Lucy could not hurry, but the train went without them. Elma remarked that if Lucy had been on her own it would probably have waited. She expected people to help her and they did.

In December she wrote to Pat Dale: 'I'd like to meet the Soviet mothers when they arrive and as a real Londoner (I lived there all my working life) I could join them in their crash trip. I think I might add to the official information e.g. Just off Holborn is a little known church where the victims to be burnt at Smithfield were allowed to stop for a 'Mass' . . . and how many folk know that in a side street off the Strand is a Roman bath still kept fresh by the original spring over which it was built? According to the route taken, no doubt other "bits" of interesting news will occur to me'. In the event Lucy insisted on joining this tourist group. She was lifted out of the minibus and carried all the way up the steps of St Paul's.

In May she was glad to welcome two East European women down to Crawley for the celebration of Peace Week there and the opening of a peace garden. The day began with a reception in the Mayor's Parlour at which Rumiana Ouzounova, one of the Mothers for Peace visitors from Bulgaria, spoke. This was followed by lunch at the Friends Meeting House for the formal opening of the peace garden. The rhodendrons and azaleas were in full bloom. A large crowd had gathered in Tilgate Park, with the trees bursting into leaf and brightly-coloured boats on the lake. Lucy walked slowly down the long half-mile path to the peace garden on the arm of the mayor. Rumiana again spoke. This

Lucy with the Mayor of Crawley at the opening of the Peace Garden in 1985.

time she told movingly of her experience in Britain as she had moved among ordinary mothers and their families. They had all shared with her their desire to bring up their families in peace—a heartfelt desire which they shared completely with Rumiana's fellow countrywomen. A stone was to be unveiled on which the words had been written by Ted Rogers, the chairman of Crawley CND. He had written:

Let us who stand here and read
remember those in the past who made

our present possible.
Now we are guardians of the future
let us ensure that generations to come can
look back to us as the people who put
an end to the nuclear arms race which
had placed the very existence of humanity
at risk.

Tony Grahame, chair of Crawley Peace Council, then led the Prayer for Peace and invited everyone to share in the common handshake of unity. A gentle walk back up the avenue took them to the spot where a maple tree was planted to remind people of the Canadian soldiers who lived there during the last war; 'a tree as a symbol of our belief in life' as Margaret Ashwell, Secretary of Crawley Peace Council, emphasized. Balloons were released with the words 'Give Peace a Chance' on them. The evening ended with music including the Pound Hill Billies singing:

Last night I had the strangest dream I'd never dreamed before,
I dreamed the world had all agreed to put an end to war . . .

This was an appropriate end to Lucy's last public engagement.

During the week after the opening of the peace garden, Lucy developed an infection. She fell in her room on Sunday afternoon, May 26th, and died shortly afterwards. She was eighty-nine.

A memorial Meeting was held for her at Ifield and another a few days later at Friends House in London to which many came, including Bruce Kent, John Cox and her other friends from CND, Mothers for Peace and the organizations with which she had worked for peace. Tributes were paid as friends recalled her indomitable spirit (Don't let's talk about why we can't do it, . . . let's do it.), her dedication, her sticking power (she could never take 'No' for an answer), her integrity, her sense of humour, and her courage.

Even a few people who found her fussy and self-important responded to her on the emotional level as they would to a favourite aunt—with great affection. One of the American mothers, Sherry Phillips, wrote: 'The witness of Marion and Lucy was quite a boost to my own peace efforts through women and the Presbyterian Church. I thank God for her witness.' It had been said that 'if only 10% of the church would work for peace it would happen. If they were all like Lucy, it would not even need 10%'. More than one person said, 'Now that she is gone, she is a good person just to think about.'

Crawley Council voted unanimously to call a road after her, Behenna Close, in the peace area at Bewbush, but of course the lasting monument to her life is the movement she and Marion started: Mothers for Peace.

This movement continues to flourish. During the summer of 1985 Sheila Ragg represented Mothers for Peace at Forum 85, the international women's assembly in Nairobi to mark the ending of the UN Decade of Women. Joyce Hallam went on WILPF's Great Peace Journey with women from all over Europe, visiting all the UN countries in Europe and asking relevant questions on peace and justice, to discover common ground on which trust could be built. The work of Mothers for Peace has extended to East European countries, especially Bulgaria, with whom the links are now very strong.

In September 1985 a unique event took place on the cliffs above Compton Bay in the Isle of Wight. A small group of women had flown in: Heidi from Boise, Idaho, USA, Janet from Canada and Marina and Keneshkan from the Soviet Union. With British women they were joining together two halves of a friendship quilt. Some of the British mothers had visited Boise the previous year. The Isle of Wight was chosen as a venue to coincide with the programme of Mothers for Peace. 'Quilting had put Boise on the map', the Boise Peace Quilt Project wrote. Now the fifteenth quilt was nearing completion they were becoming as prestigious as the Nobel prize. Presented in such diverse places as Leningrad, Greenham Common, Hiroshima and the Washington Senate, they generate the feeling that every stitch has been consciously sewn with love. They depict children's drawings, portraits of loved ones, and incorporate material of special significance to the quilter, such as a piece of wedding dress or a baby's blanket. Yet each has artistic merit. Perhaps the most 'American' is the Senators' Quilt. Consisting of fifty squares, one embroidered in each State, it bears the message:

> *Rest* beneath the warmth and weight of our hopes for the future of our children.
> *Dream* a vision of a world at peace.
> *Act* to give that vision life.

Every one of the hundred senators has been asked to spend one night under the quilt. Fifty have already done so and ten more promised.

The quilt being sewn that summer on the Isle of Wight consisted of 40 portraits of children, 20 American and 20 Soviet, featured alternately and sewn by American women. The centre panel portraying a girl with flowing hair in the shape of a dove, and the rich red and gold border depicting stylized images of the world's beauty—trees, birds, insects—had been sewn by Soviet women. The parts were pinned together on arrival in the Isle of Wight and displayed at every opportunity in such unlikely places as cafes and the Portsmouth ferry. It was planned to take the completed quilt to Geneva the following year to present it to the United Nations. And this was done.

A group of sixteen mothers left London for Moscow in October, this time including a young mother from Crawley,

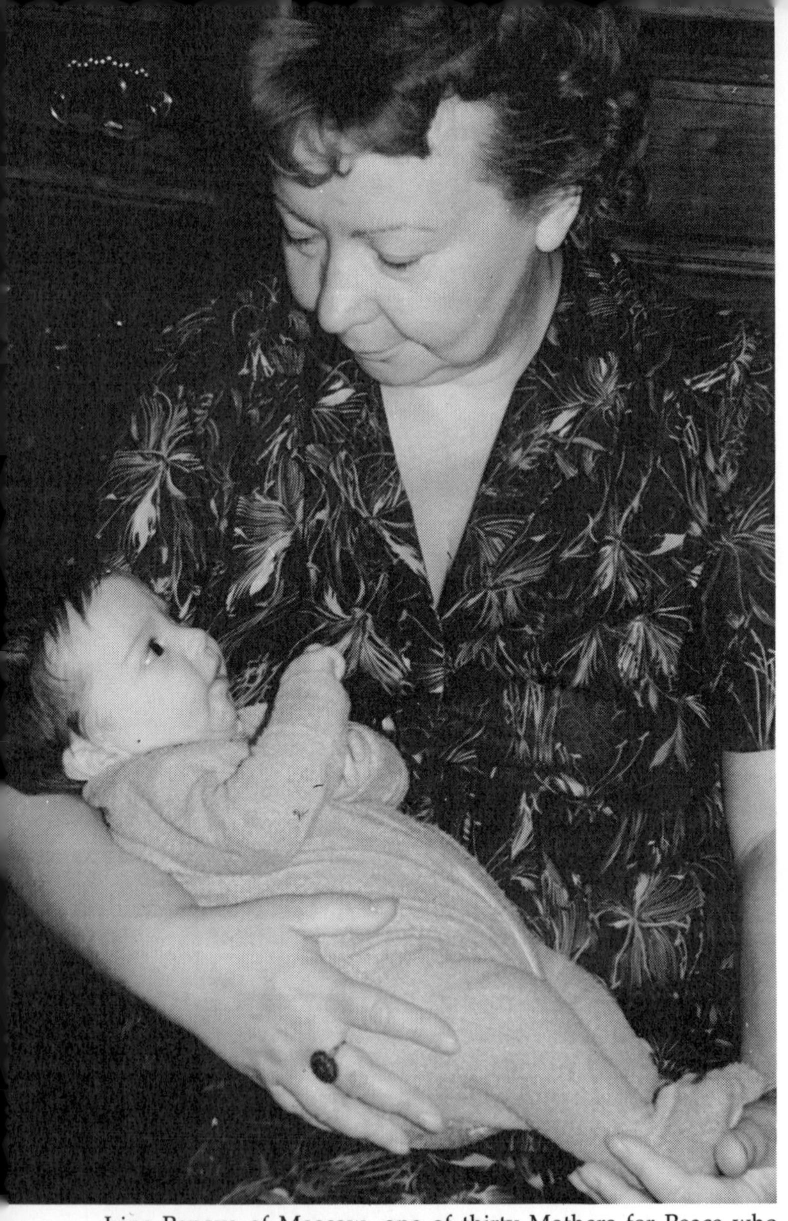

Irina Panova of Moscow, one of thirty Mothers for Peace who visited Birmingham from the USSR in June 1986, with Edward Peter Ullathorne of Cotteridge Meeting. *Photo Harriet Martin.*

Linda Townsend. She had raised her journey cost—almost £400—from sponsors and through a jumble sale and coffee morning. The ages of the mothers varied from early twenties to 'a valiant and indefatigable seventy-four', from different social and cultural backgrounds. Although some of them felt there was too much sightseeing they were able to visit a school and a kindergarten and have a round table discussion with the Soviet Women's Committee. Some of them also managed to visit Russian families and they felt very touched that they were able to relate so warmly to each other as people in spite of what their governments were telling them they should feel about each other. The most important experience of the visit was a vigil at the Piskariovskoya Cemetery in Leningrad. It was a beautiful crisp autumn day as they joined the crowds pouring into the huge garden of remembrance. Discreet evocative music filled the air. No gravestones were to be seen—only a vast area of flattened grassy mounds each with a stone slab—1942 or 1943. These were the communal graves of those who had lost their lives in the war. The mothers gathered in a semi-circle at the far end among the birch trees where they laid their 'Mothers for Peace' banner on the ground and stood in silence round it for half an hour.

Returning home they felt they had learnt a lot and had no doubt that the approach of Mothers for Peace of listening, learning and trying to understand creates trust which is the ground on which bridges can be built. Then came the equally important part of telling about their experiences to as many people as possible. Linda spoke to the British Soviet Friendship Association, Labour party groups, Friends' groups and sixth forms, for example. She found she preferred a slightly hostile audience rather than preaching to the converted.

Like a tree, the movement is growing and flowering. During the years of Lucy's life the influence not just of 'feminism' but of the female approach to life had been steadily increasing. Already we can see how attitudes change as perspectives alter. In the past, thousands of men died in battle in the belief that death in such circumstances would take them straight to heaven (as many still believe today). Yet now we can look to the statue of the Buddhist nun in Japan who, as she was about to enter heaven, heard the crying of hungry children and the suffering people of the world and turned back to help, saying that she could not go to heaven until their pain was healed.

Military leaders throughout history have accentuated the differences between nations, building up fear and hatred to encourage men to fight and die for their country. Today some of the more experienced military leaders, generals from several different nationalities, are joining together in the 'World Disarmament Campaign'. However an ex-soldier of the Vietnam war on a two-week veteran to veteran tour of the USSR organised by Earth Stewards to meet Soviet soldiers returned from Afghanistan observed:

> If anyone at all is to stop war, it will be the mothers. They are the ones with nothing to lose.[19]

It is certainly true that mothers stand to lose all that matters to them if there should be another war. It is also true that when there is a difference of ideology or culture women can find common ground partly in their very vulnerability, but mainly by giving priority to the welfare of their children through cooperation rather than competition. Under the nuclear threat this is imperative.

Such a future of course must involve justice as well as peace and in the case of oppression the situation is more complex. However, the fact remains that tyrants such as Hitler and other fascist leaders, who were emotionally twisted and immature, nevertheless had mothers, as do the arms dealers, drug traffickers and terrorists. No woman can be held responsible for the actions of her children, especially when she may be struggling to bring them up with no support, but a network of women—mothers, grandmothers, godmothers—working together to nurture whole, emotionally mature and aware human beings who are able to see life with clarity and compassion from different perspectives, surely holds out the greatest hope for the future. It is not going to happen in one generation. As Lucy warned us, it will not come easily or on the cheap, but it could be a step towards a partnership of more evolved men and women whose children can live and love and grow in the world of tomorrow as Lucy and Marion envisaged.

By the end of the last century the whole world had been explored. By the later years of this century human eyes had seen the planet as a whole from out in space. We have heard the words of the astronaut Russell Schweikart who said:

> When you go around it in an hour and a half you begin to recognize that your identity is with the whole thing. And that makes a change.
>
> You look down there and you can't imagine how many borders and boundaries you cross again and again and you don't even see them. There you are—hundreds of people killing each other over some imaginary line that you are not even aware of, that you can't see. From where you see it, the thing is a whole and it is so beautiful. You wish you could take one person in each hand and say: 'Look at it from this perspective. What's important?'
>
> You realize that on that small spot, that little blue and white thing, is everything that means anything to you. All of history and music and poetry and art and birth and love, tears, joy, games. All of it on that little spot out there that you can cover with your thumb.[20]

As the perspective of life has changed, so has the ability of women to join together in creating peace. We are grateful to Lucy and Marion for being able to see this vision and translate it into action.

# References

[1] *Willesden Chronicle*, 28 December 1962.
[2] Joseph Fleming in *Willesden Chronicle*, 18 August 1939.
[3] From *Pioneers for Peace.* Gertrude Bussey and Margaret Tims. Philadelphia, USA: Women's International League.
[4] In *Call to Women* No 35, November 1965. Edited by Margaret Curwen for the Women's Liaison Committee.
[5] Edith Simpson, 'The Tinder Box' in *The Friend*, 27 June 1980.
[6] A letter 'A Mission for Mothers' in *The Friend*, 27 June 1980.
[7] Report of Meeting for Sufferings, November 1st 1980 in *The Friend*, November 1980.
[8] *Protect and Survive* (Home Office). London: HMSO, 1980.
[9] Helen Caldicott, *Nuclear Madness: What can you do?* London: Bantam Books, 1981.
[10] Martin Luther King quoted in *Bridgebuilders for Peace.* London: Quaker Peace & Service, 1983 from *Strength to Love.* London: Fontana, p. 52.
[11] In *Tears and Rainbows.* Leeds: Mothers for Peace, 1983.
[12] Ibid.
[13] From *Greenham Women Everywhere*, ed. Alice Cook and Gwyn Kirk. London: Pluto Press, 1983.
[14] *Tears and Rainbows.* op. cit.
[15] Pete Seeger's song quoted in *Tears and Rainbows* op.cit.
[16] *Mothers for Peace: Spring and Autumn Visits to USA and USSR 1984* ed. Pat Dale. Leeds: Mothers for Peace, 1985.
[17] John Hersey, *Hiroshima.* Harmondsworth, Middx: Penguin Books, 1978.
[18] *Mothers for Peace* op. cit., pp. 21–22.
[19] John Lyon quoted in 'Best of Enemies' by Peter Naysmith in the *Observer Magazine*, 12 February 1989.
[20] Russell Schweikart quoted in *The Awakening Earth* by Peter Russell. London: Routledge & Kegan Paul, 1982.

# *Further Reading*

I have found the following books especially helpful in my research:

*Bridge Builders for Peace,* published for Mothers for Peace by Quaker Peace & Service, London, 1983.

*Tears and Rainbows,* Mothers for Peace. Leeds: Mothers for Peace, 1983.

*Mothers for Peace,* Mothers for Peace. Leeds: Mothers for Peace, 1984.

*The CND Story,* ed. John Minnion and Philip Bolsover. London: Allison and Busby, 1983.

*Greenham Women Everywhere,* ed. Alice Cook and Gwyn Kirk. London: Pluto Press, 1983.

*Pioneers for Peace,* Gertrude Bussey and Margaret Tims. Philadelphia, USA: Women's International League for Peace and Freedom, 1980.

*Most Dangerous Women. Feminist Peace Campaigners of the Great War,* Anne Wiltsher. London: Pandora Press, 1985.

*I Renounce War. Story of Peace Pledge Union,* Sybil Morrison. London: Sheppard Press, 1962.

*Bloody Conchie . . . ! a conscientious objector looks back at World War 2,* Alex Bryan. London: Quaker Home Service, 1986.

*Mary Hughes: a friend to all in need,* Hugh Pyper. London: Quaker Home Service, 1983.

*Yesteryears – School, Work and Leisure,* ed. and published by Sylvia Bond, 31 Holnesdale Road, Highgate, London, 1979.